BIG Applause for *Who Are Yo*

"Being BIG is one of the most imp_____
effective. This book shows you how to do it."
—David Cohen, General Counsel of a Professional Football Franchise

"The game has changed in our industry and our company in recent years. This book makes game changing leadership easy. BIG makes it easy to stay true to your values and lead with integrity."

—Katherine Le, President, Stearns Lending

"We all have times when we feel BIG and when we feel small. Read this book and recover to BIG more easily."

—Nina Green, Executive at a Fortune 50 Company

"BIG has allowed me to step into being a more strategic leader, particularly through some periods of substantial change. My team, my company and my family have all been the beneficiaries of the messages contained in this book. Read it today."

—David Conley, CFO, Orora North America
(Formerly AMCOR Packaging and Distribution Company)

"My seatmate on a flight the other day was a successful and intriguing woman in her own right. In talking about our hopes and dreams she said, 'I've found that I can get anything I want accomplished in 48 hours or less. My problem is that it takes six months for my head and heart to agree on what that is.' Is the battle between your head and heart holding you back from being BIG? A simple question worth asking, that this book answers."

—Joanna Bloor, Vice President, Pandora

"*The move to the digital economy is here. Successful leaders in this monumental transition will be those who are willing and able to explore new ways of working. Don't miss your opportunity to play BIG!*"

—Colleen Berube, Vice President, IT Business Services, Adobe Inc.

"*This world needs more leaders and BIG is a prerequisite for success and significance. Allan and Kimberly make a compelling case that your greatest value lies in your most authentic leadership and that from there you have everything you need to change the world.*"

—Henry and Karen Kimsey-House, Co-Founders of CTI (The Coaches Training Institute)

"*The messages from* Who Are You . . . When You Are BIG? *helped me rediscover who I am and live with confidence, gratitude, humility, and joy. I was able to peel back my layers of self-doubt, insecurity, and fears. I have let go of the inner voice that hampered my ability to be my best self, take risks, and make bold moves. I value the time I need to take to know myself and listen to the heartbeat of my soul. As a leader, I trust myself first, acknowledge the incredible privilege I have to do the work we do, live my values, and have fun in the process!*"

—Paula Alderson, President and CEO, Hospice by the Sea, Inc.

"*Kimberly and Allan have distilled what it takes to be a truly confident leader. Their book will help you understand your own strengths and abilities and promote your team's confidence and positivity. I strongly recommend their straightforward approach to achieve your best, overcome your inner critic, and bring out the best of everyone on your team.*"

—Chris Paskach, Partner and National Practice Leader, Forensic Technology KPMG, LLP *(Retired)*

"BIG is transformational in moving you towards thriving both professionally and personally that results in truly "authentic" leadership. You are in it for you, and it benefits all."

—Ruth Papazian, Chief Marketing Officer & Head of Business Development, HD Vest Financial Services

"Let your genie out of the bottle. Learn how BIG you already are and let the others simply see the real you. An incredibly positive and empowering read. "

—Tom Bang, CEO, Bluestep/Bridgegate Health

"BIG reminds me that my ability and my compassion have a positive impact on my daughter, my team and my community."

—Jessica K. Cervantez, Firefighter, Camp Pendleton Fire Department

"I was exposed to the concept of Who Are You . . . When You Are BIG *while going through the Executives in Transition Boot Camp. While in transition, it is easy to lose confidence in yourself. But by stepping back and reflecting on all of those instances when you are BIG, you realize how capable you are and what it looks like and feels like when you are BIG so you can capture those moments to share and serve as focal points for your ongoing success. This exercise helped ground me in my BIG. Thank you, Kimberly and Allan."*

—Ken Sobaski, Operating Partner, Alpine Investors

"Game on! This book will coach and challenge you to bring your BIG to every endeavor."

—Sarah Booth, Director of Retail Marketing, ASICS America Corporation

Who Are You...When You Are BIG?

Who Are You...When You Are BIG?

ALLAN MILHAM
KIMBERLY ROUSH

Advantage®

Copyright © 2014 by Allan Milham & Kimberly Roush

All rights reserved. No part of this book may be used or reproduced in any manner whatsoever without prior written consent of the author, except as provided by the United States of America copyright law.

Published by Advantage, Charleston, South Carolina.
Member of Advantage Media Group.

ADVANTAGE is a registered trademark and the Advantage colophon is a trademark of Advantage Media Group, Inc.

Printed in the United States of America.

ISBN: 978-1-59932-455-5
LCCN: 2014936936

This publication is designed to provide accurate and authoritative information in regard to the subject matter covered. It is sold with the understanding that the publisher is not engaged in rendering legal, accounting, or other professional services. If legal advice or other expert assistance is required, the services of a competent professional person should be sought.

Advantage Media Group is proud to be a part of the Tree Neutral® program. Tree Neutral offsets the number of trees consumed in the production and printing of this book by taking proactive steps such as planting trees in direct proportion to the number of trees used to print books. To learn more about Tree Neutral, please visit **www.treeneutral.com**. To learn more about Advantage's commitment to being a responsible steward of the environment, please visit **www.advantagefamily.com/green**

Advantage Media Group is a publisher of business, self-improvement, and professional development books and online learning. We help entrepreneurs, business leaders, and professionals share their Stories, Passion, and Knowledge to help others Learn & Grow. Do you have a manuscript or book idea that you would like us to consider for publishing? Please visit **advantagefamily.com** or call **1.866.775.1696**.

This book is dedicated to those who are ready to . . .

Be BIG
Live BIG
Lead BIG!

Courageously release what already lies within you.
Join us to inspire even more BIGness in the world!

CONTENTS

ACKNOWLEDGEMENTS

Allan's:

Writing a book is a team sport and in every team—
there are stand-outs who help make the magic happen.

In the case of BIG, I want to acknowledge my wife,
Janis, who for over twenty years has served as a portal
for me to jump into my full potential. You have been
and are my biggest cheerleader.

To my co-author, Kimberly, for the courage to cut
away from the herd and find your BIG, allowing for
thousands to be inspired by your commitment to
follow your heart.

And to the hundreds of clients over the years
through my coaching business who have elevated my
game, allowing me to do God's work with such ease.

Kimberly's:

My heart is filled with gratitude for the many miracles
that have come together while writing this book.

My husband, Steve, has been both my rock and the

wind beneath my wings through it all. Your support behind the scenes is amazing and I will be forever grateful for having been lucky enough to be your wife.

My brother's courage has inspired me to fully live from my heart.

My mom and dad who have always loved me, believed in me and told me anything was possible.

My co-hosts, Christi Haley Stover and Tenny Poole, have played BIG with me in our Boot Camp for Executives in Transition. It was in those sessions that I came to realize this was too BIG not to share more broadly.

The Boot Campers and clients who have written BIG statements and allowed me to witness their magnificence emerge creating a geyser of BIGness.

My Bobcat tribe, who has moved me from "me" to "we" on many fronts and held me with fierce love.

Finally—Allan, my coach and co-author, you've asked the questions that have changed my life and called me forth into Bold Move territory, again and again. This book would not have been possible without you. You brought BIGness to this project beyond what I ever could have imagined.

The secret of the champions

by Allan Milham

The hearts, hundreds of them, pulsated neon red in the darkness. I was 13 years old, clutching a microphone in the crowded auditorium of my school, and as I looked out from the stage at my audience, I could see what appeared to be glass hearts glowing brightly through the clothing of everyone there. I felt deeply moved, as if whatever I was saying was truly touching those hearts.

It was a powerful little dream that I would not recall until three decades later. When it came back to me in my forties, the dream was as vivid as it was in junior high. By then I was a consultant and senior leadership performance coach, in the business of trying to touch hearts—but for so very long I hadn't had a clue about what I should be doing. That dream seemed to have been a glimmer of things to come, a harbinger of possibilities. I feel today that I was meant to serve as a catalyst for leaders and others who are hungry to achieve their potential. As a coach, author, and keynote speaker, I look forward to inspiring an ever-wider audience. I want people to see their greater purpose as they find the powerful "what's next" in their lives.

I started my coaching business in 1998 with a desire to work with top performers—those who have a motivation and drive to have a fulfilling life, to move forward versus backwards, to look for opportunities and then to go to the next level.

In graduate school, I worked in the San Francisco office of the global career management consulting firm, Drake Beam Morin, where I had the privilege to work with executives whom I thought met that definition of top performer. I was the only one in my grad school class who was not going into psychotherapy. I found that I liked working with ambitious people who needed a boost in life. There are times in life's journey when we're not meant to be lone rangers, when a partnership allows for greater growth.

Our firm was a sponsor of the 1996 Olympics in Atlanta and provided career-transition resources to bright and accomplished men and women who, in their early twenties, were facing the big question: Now what? I had the opportunity to work with a couple of them who were in the San Francisco Bay Area.

That was a milestone in my career. From a young age,

I had been interested in the development of human potential. I had long been curious about why some people keep moving up the ladder of life while others never seem to reach for the next rung. Some soar, and some plateau—but why?

I was in my thirties at the time, a decade older than these young Olympians, these best of the best among the world's athletes. How were they able to do what they had done? Yes, they had an athletic agility, but beyond that I wondered how they endured the pressure. The ones I worked with were individual competitors, not part of a team, and so they had performed before millions while representing their country. People are passionate about their country's athletes and get intensely invested in the winning and the losing. How had these athletes focused under such demands?

Our inner conversations

To learn, I asked—and I listened. And I heard how each of them was aware of an inner conversation between fear and hope, between anxiety and confidence. They had effectively managed those voices and concluded: "Hey, I'm well trained, and I've worked all my life for this moment. I'm good to go." By listening only to the positive voices and shutting the negative talk out, they had attained a state of mind in which they felt invincible. They didn't just go for the gold; they knew they could get it. They believed.

One young female Olympian seemed puzzled at first when I asked her about that inner drive. Her belief in herself was so inherent and subconscious that she didn't realize how important a role it had played in her success. She knew instinctively how to manage those voices. Positivity was just part of who she was. As they say in the South: "When you order breakfast, you don't have to ask for grits. They just come with it." For some people—and far too few—positivity just comes with it.

That attitude struck me. I have seen adults two or three times older than these Olympians who have never learned to manage that voice of negativity that hogs the microphone, droning out messages of, "I'm an imposter—I just got lucky," "I'm afraid," or "I can't do this." Some die under that influence, never to make the most of themselves.

Working with the Olympians was a profound experience, and it led me to look through the lens of top performers for perspectives on how to manage those internal messages. Who will we allow to step to the microphone of our lives, and what will we have them say? Certainly, a lot has been written on the topic of managing those inner voices.

Why not, I wondered, take that concept and apply it to my work? I began to do so at the career management-consulting firm, and then, in the late 1990s, I launched my coaching business, where I began working that concept intently with my clients, who were top performers. I remember feeling a bit nervous—like, "Wow, this is a bit out there"—but as I completed my engagements, I was struck by how often my clients cited those inner conversations. They put a high value on how the coaching had made them aware of the need for techniques to manage those voices for greater results and fulfillment.

We don't necessarily eradicate the negative voice—it just comes as part of the human condition—but we certainly can manage it and quiet it so that we can reach for the bigger things in life. Learning to control that negative voice is transformational. In addition, learning to listen to your inner champion within is where BIG comes alive. It is a pillar of the message that we want to share in this book—the discovery of who you are when you are BIG.

Disposition isn't destiny

I have had the opportunity to participate in a program with Martin Seligman, former president of the American Psychological Association and head of the psychology department at the University of Pennsylvania. He is considered by many to be the founding father of the relatively new field of positive psychology. In the coaching program that he facilitated, I was fascinated by his views on our predisposition to being optimistic or pessimistic. We are born with a predisposition, but it is a trainable trait. We can shift that orientation.

As you can imagine, those with a pessimistic bent will be taking a different pathway than will those who are inherently optimistic. When you have attained the latter mindset, those negative voices quiet down. Coaching professionals use a variety of terms for that negative voice—"saboteur" is used by CTI (The Coaches Training Institute). Some call it "the gremlin," "inner critic," or "the critter." You will find us using all those nicknames, at times—in fact, we encourage clients to come up with their own. But by any name, it's far from rosy.

Between optimism and pessimism is the "realist," the image that many people have of themselves. "Well, I'm actually a realist," they will say if anyone asks which way they lean. Those who define themselves as realists often will deny that there is a negative voice within them. They simply believe they see the world for what it is.

Those three orientations—optimist, pessimist, and realist—are part of the human continuum. Each is a common characteristic, and none precludes success. Sometimes people wonder whether they can ever be a success if they are fundamentally pessimistic. Take heart: There is a way. Regardless of your inner outlook, you can reach greatness. You can be BIG. And it starts with awareness of those messages you send to yourself.

A calling for coaches

My coauthor, Kimberly Roush, and I both have been certified through CTI (www.thecoaches.com), one of the most reputable coach training organizations in the world. In addition, I have earned, and Kimberly is in the application process for, the Master Certified Coach (MCC) designation—the highest level of certification awarded by the International Coach Federation. It is considered by many to be the PhD of the coaching industry; there are only 650 MCCs in the world. The ICF has defined rigorous standards and ethical guidelines for the profession. (available at www.coachfederation.org).

In 2012, there were just short of 50,000 non-sports-related coaches globally in the coaching industry, which only started to become recognized in the late 1980s. In 2013, the industry moved toward $2 billion in annual revenue. That's powerful growth in a little over two decades. Numerous articles in the *Harvard Business*

Review and elsewhere have reported that the bottom line results, the return on investment, show that the field is far from a fad. It has gained an amazing amount of traction.

When people worked decades in the same job, they had advisors and resources within the organization to help them along. Today, people don't stay put like that. They're not working for the same few people their entire career. They don't have the same people watching them and grooming them. It is now up to individuals to take a lot more responsibility for their own development.

That's a particularly acute need at the executive level. As they come up through most any organization, most receive training and development all the way along. And then all of a sudden, they become an executive and either they're too busy to attend those programs or they aren't offered for that level.

Many executives advanced because they were always interested in personal development and growth or gaining new expertise. Now that stops, as if it is presumed that they know it all. As executives, they risk becoming stale in their personal development. As executive coaches, we remedy that.

After my early success in the coaching field, I had a vision of getting the message out to a greater audience instead of just working with perhaps a few dozen people a year. I had long desired to become a professional speaker, and writing a book seemed a prerequisite.

In 2007, I co-authored *Bold Moves*, with Shayla Roberts. For the first time, I articulated in writing how I went about my coaching. The book was designed part novel, part fable, and part readers' log, with practical applications. The fable told of three tadpoles named Jump, Croak, and Plop who awaken the nighttime creatures in a marsh. Of the three, it was Jump who could see a world of possibilities beyond the marsh. *His* dreams were in Technicolor®. The fable intertwines with a tale of a visionary CEO looking for Bold Move makers to help run his organization. He begins working with a professional coach.

The book broadened the audience for the message that I had been delivering to clients for several years. It was while I was writing my earlier book that Kimberly made her own Bold Move to leave a prestigious role in "Big 4" public accounting to pursue a coaching career, and she has been a strong advocate of that book among her own clients.

Now, with this book, we further develop the audience. Kimberly came to me with the idea of publishing a compendium of BIG stories she had collected, suggesting that I coauthor it, because BIG was a concept that she had learned from me. I wouldn't be interested, I told her, unless we turned the project into a Bold Move—a platform for speaking, creating a movement, and more. She agreed, and we, together, began thinking like Olympians in this project.

I had been working with Kimberly in her career development, and my hope was to continue inspiring my client to greatness. If she wanted to write a book about thinking big, then I wanted her to think BIG about the book. My first book had described three types of mindsets for "move makers"—the "barely" move maker, the "brash" move maker, and the "bold" move maker. She had clearly demonstrated that she was the latter.

I operated in brashness much of my life. Fear and doubt kept creeping in, until I understood that I had a real choice. I had been an optimistic kid. In anyone's life, situations can trigger apprehensions, but today I have a far greater ability to manage those feelings than I did when I was younger. I know—and Kimberly knows— that there is a better way. You can wake up with a new outlook, engage in work differently, have better relationships, and be a more powerful parent. We must not let ourselves be consumed by negativity. Yes, troubles and worries are part of life—but we get a choice on how we will react to them. Which pathway do you want to take?

In each of us, an Olympian

What, then, does it mean to be BIG? It means defining that state of mind where your inner Olympian lives. You don't become instantly and consistently BIG by flicking on a light switch. Think of it instead as a dimmer switch that dials up or down. So much will determine your level of intensity at any particular moment, and that's all right—so long as the current is still running. If you sense your light needs to be brighter, you can turn up the dial at any time. You can step into your BIGness. From there, Bold Moves are possible . . . if you are ready. The key is "ready"—you need not have actually made that move before you consider yourself BIG. It's the reverse: You need to be BIG before making that move.

I have seen Kimberly step into her own BIGness—and in her own practice, she has taken the BIG concept to hundreds of executives through a boot camp that she co-facilitates and hosts with colleagues from two other companies. It's a free program, two or three hours a week for a month, for executives in transition. I am proud that a central part of that boot camp is based on the concept that I use, and that I asked her as my client, "Who are you when you are BIG?"

Kimberly and her co-facilitators ask their boot campers to write a narrative of who they are when they feel that way. The results show clearly how that question empowers and propels. Those who answer that question effectively will have a blueprint for their success. Imagine the power of reading it daily, over coffee or before a meeting or interview, as a reminder of who you truly are.

Your inner critic may be saying, "This is all very nice, but I'm no Olympian"—but there is an Olympian within everyone who is hungry to go for the gold. You feel small if you believe that others are better than you, or that they received the greater share of life's gifts and breaks. Every human being at some point has felt a flash of inferiority, as if he or she didn't belong in the room with people of such magnitude. Those who succeed manage to turn that flash into a spark. It's an opportunity to grow.

If you are yearning for something—whether it is more fulfillment in your work, a meaningful life, or a Bold Move—you can go for it. You can gain the self-confidence and self-esteem to make it happen, and help is all around you, more than ever before. Never dismiss your possibilities. Your heart whispers to you. Answer it. When you do, the rest will seem effortless.

When I am BIG . . .

I'm sleepless. I can't stop thinking about all the projects I want to start, the people I want to connect with, and the books I want to read. **I feel like a teenager.**

I take the wheel. I open the moon roof, I increase the volume of the radio, and I sing out loud as if the world was mine. **I feel invincible.**

I speak up. I trust my instinct, I don't fear controversy, and I express my opinion without filters. **I feel authentic.**

I go for what I want. I stay focused until I reach the final line, no matter how long it takes and the obstacles I encounter. **I feel like an Olympian.**

I lean in. I find the "white" spaces, I take ownership, and I make it happen. **I feel like an entrepreneur.**

I entertain. I invite amazing people and I craft a memorable experience for them: great food, French wine, and jazz in the background. **I feel like an Iron Chef.**

I'm in balance. I take care of my health, and I'm available for my family, my friends, and my team. **I feel in harmony.**

I take off. I fly with my boyfriend to vibrant cities of the world where we get inspired and dream big about us. **I feel brand new.**

**— SYLVIE FELX,
Sr. Manager, IT Brand Communication
and Transformation, Adobe Inc.**

CHAPTER 1

What's the **BIG** deal?

I f you could only see what we have seen in our coaching businesses about human potential, you would believe even more in yourself.

You see, we get to witness the inherent greatness inside our clients emerge all the time. It never fails. The thrill of seeing people shed fear and doubt, anxiety, stress, feeling overwhelmed, or the defeatist mindset and instead step into incredible self-confidence and self-esteem is magical. It doesn't come from a place of big ego but rather from a place of inner knowing and purpose. And not everyone comes from a place of deficiency in his or her own mind. Some come from a place of great self-confidence and view themselves as highly success-ful, yet long for something more. It's as if they wake up one day and say, "Gosh, I've worked hard all along, I've achieved great things, I've got the title, the money, the company—but I thought it would mean more than this. I thought I would be happier. When does it get easier?"

Some feel like they've been running on a hamster wheel. It just doesn't help to run faster or to build your endurance so you can run longer. What if you could change that hamster wheel into a Ferris wheel where you could always see the big picture and enjoy the view as it goes around? What if the key to doing that lay largely within you—in your perspective or your beliefs about the wheel or about yourself? What if, metaphorically, the wheel is within you and you get to make a choice every day to play small on the hamster wheel or to play big like a Ferris wheel? What if the Ferris wheel represented the core of your personal authentic leadership based on your values and your very own definition of personal success? What is your brand of what it means "when you are BIG?"

That's the big deal

So many people come to believe that the key to their success lies in something outside of themselves. "If only I had that degree," or "If only I had that job," or, "If only I had that relationship." It's time to hit the mute button on those voices. You have everything you need today to be BIG and your answers lie within, waiting to be revealed.

Often, people co-opt others' beliefs and values, as if they were commodities that could be assigned. "Uncle

Jack says I shouldn't think that way about it," they will comment, or, "What would my mother say if I did that?" To be a good leader, you must tap into your own core values. If you are living and acting out of sync with those values, then your life and career are likely to go adrift. To navigate, you need to take control of the rudder.

"Who are you when you are BIG?" is the fundamental question that we implore you to answer. What is the nature of your innate greatness? We are not asking you to tell us, "I am BIG when . . .," and list past victories, or your set of conditions that must be met. Rather, tell us what you are like when you clearly are feeling BIG. The question gets to the heart of what emanates from the inside rather than what is imposed from the outside.

When you recognize that greatness is inside you, just waiting to come out, you are on the path to discovery. You are learning to design your life to fulfill your potential. You are on your way to becoming your best.

Watching people become fully empowered is magical. It is a privilege to see our clients, day by day, move past where they were stuck. Having remembered, finally, who they really are, they step into themselves and out into the world.

We want to broaden that magic beyond what we see

every day with our clients. As executive coaches, we each work with many people who are eager to take their level of leadership higher. Our focus is on business leaders, but the principles we espouse are universal, and we hope to reach a much wider audience.

> *Success requires more than the line items on a resume. You must be more than good at something. You must be true to yourself.*

Those principles, in essence, are about human potential, about making the most of life. They apply as well to the single mom or dad struggling to pay the bills, to the couple forging a future together, to the child eager to make friends in a new school, to the young person feeling his or her way in a first job, and to the teenager facing more pressures than grown-ups can even imagine. Those are just a few. Life happens to us all.

We have learned in our experience that those who wish to develop as people and leaders need to embrace this concept of their BIGness—of discovering who they really are when they are at their best. Success requires more than the line items on a resume. You must be more than good at something. You must be true to yourself.

Who we are, whom we serve

Let us more formerly introduce ourselves: We are Kimberly Roush and Allan Milham, with extensive experience in working with executives who are ready to reach for that higher level. Our clients are senior leaders, rising stars in their organization, or they may be unemployed and in transition. You need not have a job to pursue your dreams.

Our practices are separate—in fact, on opposite coasts. Respectively, they are All-Star Executive Coaching, based in Orange County, California, and Bold Moves Enterprises, based in Washington, D.C. Our emphasis, however, is the same: We offer tailored programs specific to the needs of executives who are looking for new energy, inspiration, and direction. They range from Fortune 100 C-level executives to solo entrepreneurs. Some are leaders newly promoted, some are yearning to get to the next level, and some desire to reinvent their careers.

We work with very talented people who are clearly high performers and who have sought out coaching so that they can reach even greater levels. They're looking for something more, and they're ready for something more. "More" may not mean a more impressive title or more money. It might be more confidence in the job that they're doing, or more balance in their lives, or more fulfillment in their work, or more fun so that it doesn't feel like drudgery. They may feel stuck. They are in search of something and might not even know what it is—or they think they know, but that's not what it is at all. We try to discover that up front: What is this really all about?

Our clients aren't necessarily looking to change professions or jobs or their career path in any way. They may do that—as we both did as we found our own passions—but it is not what most people do. Most search and find meaning and fulfillment, and fun, in the jobs that they have now. Just because they are unsatisfied does not mean they need to bail out of a job, any more than they would bail out of a marriage or relationship without deep consideration of the options and consequences.

In addition to coaching our clients, we continue to work with professional coaches ourselves and invest annually in our own personal and professional development. In addition to our extensive coach training though CTI, we both participated in CTI's one-year leadership program. It's a series of four week-long retreats that aim to help leaders understand why they were put on this planet and reignite their hunger to live fully and not just settle. Participants are encouraged to march to their own drumbeat, not to someone else's, and then join in partnership with others so that they can share with the world what they uniquely have to offer. For more information

on this extraordinary leadership program, visit www.
thecoaches.com. In writing this book and in broadening
our audience, we hope to continue to fulfill the ideals of
that program. This is our drumbeat, and we invite you
to join us.

A boot camp boost

Besides working with rising stars, for more than six years
All-Star Executive Coaching has collaborated to pay it
forward by offering a boot camp for stars who may feel
they have fallen. They are executives in transition, most
in their forties, fifties, or sixties. They never thought they
would be unemployed. They have been recruited from
one position to the next. They're good at what they do,
and yet they have lost their job title. It feels like identity
theft. They may feel dispirited, small, "less than."

Looking for a boost, they tend to focus on their resume—
all those things they've done. But in the job market,
what they have done sounds remarkably similar to what
so many others have done. What they come to discover
in the boot camp is that what makes them most hireable
is who they are inside. They haven't lost their leadership
ability, and that's what companies are looking for.

They come to understand the compelling difference
between "What I *can* do" and "What I *want* to do" for a

meaningful, purposeful life. A research study once asked a thousand HR professionals what was most important in hiring—whether the prospective employee *can* do the work (skills, competencies), whether the prospect is motivated to do the work (will, interest), and *how* do they fit in the culture. Over-whelmingly, the respondents chose the latter. In interviews, they wanted to hear whether prospects were compatible with their culture. What were they looking for? If the right values are in place, the skills can be learned—but not the other way around. In other words, they were impressed when interviewees knew who they were when they were BIG. When they could see that, they knew whether that person would fit.

> **If the right values are in place, the skills can be learned—but not the other way around.**

Americans tend to define themselves through their jobs, but that's not the core of who they are. A common phenomenon in America is the question that often is first spoken in a social gathering: "What do you . . . *do*?" In many other countries, people tell you where they hail from, or they talk proudly of their children or grandchildren, or they share that they enjoy landscape painting—and oh, yes, they work at such-and-such company.

When you identify yourself by your job, it does indeed feel as if you are losing your identity when you become unsure of yourself, things are not going the way you want, or your position is stripped away by the economy or whatever powers that be. But when you tap into who you truly are when you are BIG, you no longer feel like a victim or that something has been done to you. You regain your power, and you can move forward—and that is the new freedom that a boot camper can experience.

Your authentic leadership

The nature of power and leadership is not etched in stone—there is no single definition of how best to influence people or how to command respect and take authority. Think of Winston Churchill and Mahatma Gandhi, for example. Both were great leaders, hugely influential, widely quoted, but with far different approaches. Some great leaders gain influence by confident command. Others gain influence by persistent and quiet inspiration. All great leaders gain their power from being themselves, not from projecting some false image.

If you aspire to be a better leader, it's high time to begin the journey. It's time to recognize and develop your own unique style. It's time to make sure you are on track to an authentic life and career.

In childhood, we first wonder what we will do when we grow up, and the question gets louder and louder as the pressure for an answer builds through high school and into college. Sometimes it isn't answered until years later, if ever. But if you allow yourself to be authentic, it is likely that you will grow into the career that was meant for you.

As a wise observer once said, "Be yourself. Everyone else is taken."

BIG is a state of mind

One of the key principles of BIG is that it is a state of mind. In Bold Moves, it is referred to as your "Optimal Operating State," in which you tap into your core values. Unfortunately, the external world so often overwhelms the inner world that many people are far from optimal. In a world missing its

> **One of the key principles of BIG is that it is a state of mind.**

potential, consider the vast cost of the missed opportunities. Strong leaders can have a huge impact on that reality.

Surveys on quality of life in today's world find that feelings of prosperity, happiness, and well-being are at an all-time low—despite high education levels and all the technology that is supposed to make our lives better. One out of ten Americans are on some form of anti-depression medication, with prescription spending currently at about $325 billion a year. In a happiness index that ranked fifty countries, Americans ranked seventeenth. A Gallup study found that by the end of 2012, on average only 30 percent of the workforce reports being engaged in their work. Further, their study showed that 52 percent are "not engaged" and 18 percent are "actively disengaged!" The disinterest and unhappiness are affecting performance: Gallup estimates that actively disengaged employees cost the United States alone $450 to $550 billion in lost productivity each year. Almost half of us report that we eat to improve our mood. Americans are among the most obese people in the world, with one of the highest divorce rates.

Yet, many of us yearn for better. Consider this: A Harvard course on positive psychology became one of the university's most popular courses. The instructor, Tal Ben-Shahar, wrote a brilliant book about it, *Happier*. He talks about the four states that we can fall into—one of which, the rat racers, describes most leaders in today's culture. Many people move through life with a "head-down-plow-through" mentality, hoping that someday when they reach all of their goals they will find happiness. As a result, they sacrifice and postpone happiness for later. Ben-Sharar's research explains that once they get "there," wherever that is, happiness often times is not what they find. His course and his book offer a perspective of living in the here and now, enjoying the journey instead of just looking for rewards.

Today, amid so many choices and so much uncertainty, the pressure to achieve a standardized measure of success is greater than ever. We are bombarded daily with a minimum of 3,000 external messages telling us who and what we should be. To be BIG requires us to be able to put on armor against the external messages and look inward to find our own true path. This can be a challenge, as some will be stuck in not knowing which path to take. Others charge down a path not knowing where it will lead. Yet, some have a road map to get them down the right path.

Making moves: barely, brash, bold move makers

The mindset—barely, brash, or bold can make all the difference.

Barely move makers dwell in fear and doubt, in anxiety and hopelessness. They become apathetic and unplugged, living through other people's experiences. They are barely getting by, just punching in and punching out.

Barely move makers add little value, and that mindset can bring down a family, a team, an organization.

Brash move makers also dwell in fear, doubt, and anxiety, but do so with an energy that demands attention. They can be like a bad virus. The brashness often comes from immaturity, insecure ego, or low self-esteem. The energy can mask the apprehension and scarcity thinking, and that can make it all the more damaging. Be warned: That mindset can ripple out from the leadership to affect dozens, hundreds, even millions of others. Think of former Fortune 500 companies that have crumbled due to brash leadership or the wars that have raged around the world. The brash mindset can expand wildly.

Top performers often are prone to the brash mindset at times. All of us can fall into it, in our families, on the job, with our teams. We see it all the time in business—those leaders who never would win a congeniality award because of their need for control or to win at all costs. They are vulnerable, and their performance is hit-or-miss. Something can trigger a bad day in all of us, but what is important is to notice when it is happening; otherwise, that fear, doubt, and anxiety can hold us hostage and, worse yet, those around us.

By contrast, **Bold** move makers operate from a place of hope and possibility. There's a sense of excitement and adventure. Positivity prevails, and that, too, can spread like a virus, but a good virus that infects an entire organization—whether a corporation or a family or a community. People want to be around Bold Move makers, because they are inspiring and empowering. They get results.

You might say that the Bold Move maker is running like finely tuned machinery. Often, we will ask clients what conditions need to be in place for them to be performing at their best. What gives them the right mindset and attitude? Defining those elements is essential if they are to recognize when they are missing their mark.

We often see people in our practices who feel stuck on where to go next or how to get there—be it in their role as a leader, their career, or their lives. Before, opportunities always seemed to present themselves, whether a job, a promotion, a challenging project, company growth, etc. Not anymore. It's often a humbling time for them, but they soon learn that it is also a fortuitous time. They are finally about to find themselves and align with their values. They are about to find what isn't working and get unstuck. And it's none too soon. Today's world, fraught with issues and demands, needs all of us operating at our potential. It's not overreaching to say that our very survival is at stake. Now more than ever, we need to harness our BIGness—to play the BIGger game. Leaders need to set the example so that others can be inspired to play a BIGger game, too.

When you're aligned to your true self, you are more likely to fit in wherever you go. That's because you know who you value yourself to be and stop trying to play who you think you should be. We hear that all the time from clients in our practices: "I should do this, I should be that." They're *should*-ing all over themselves. We coach them to instead tap into what they truly are "wanting."

> **Leaders need to set the example so that others can be inspired to play a BIGger game, too.**

We want to get people in front of the mirror. So many people base their lives on others' expectations. It might be rooted in childhood. If you do this, you're a good boy. If you do that, you're a good girl. This is how you will be worthy of love. That is how you will make something of yourself. There's no malicious intent. Depression-era parents, for example, often imparted hard-learned survival skills. The advice might actually be sound—but what matters is what comes from your own heart. When you look inward, you finally can move past stuck—onward and upward.

That's why the question. "Who am I when I am BIG?" is so powerful. It allows us to pause amid the noise and naysayers and commercial static. We can be what we have not allowed ourselves to be. We can escape those voices of, "This is what you must do to succeed," or "Don't do that or you will fail." It's not too late to change. We have the resources. We feel the yearning. It's time to go for it. Imagine the ripple effect if people start thinking BIG regarding their families, their jobs, and their communities.

One man who came in for career coaching was a medical doctor in his thirties. His father had been a doctor, too, who apparently had issued a prescription for his son's career path. It was a sad story: The man had invested fifteen years or so in med school, residency, and special-ization. It seemed the outer world had taken control of his destiny, and he was miserable but, fortunately, he was able to begin listening internally and turn things around.

A lot of people get on the wrong track—not just in their careers, but in their family lives and their relationships, or to whatever they find themselves devoting their time. They may find themselves married with children and debt, and wondering just who charted their course. It takes courage to take control of the rudder for yourself, but it is not impossible. And when you take control, you may find that you need only a light touch to make things right.

As coaches, both of us have worked with many executives who made adjustments in their careers. In our own careers, we each took major turns—and they were right turns, not off to the left somewhere. But the change need not be dramatic. Often, people have been deliberate about their career choice and love their field; they just have gotten caught up in a part of it that they don't like. Sometimes, it's just a matter of getting back to their roots and remembering what they love about their job and allowing themselves to focus far more on that. You don't necessarily have to make the BIG right turn and completely change what you're doing. You're not necessarily on the wrong path; you may just have hit a rough stretch or don't know exactly where you are.

> *Whether you need wholesale change or a tweak to your pattern, the power of the question will serve you well:*
>
> *"Who are you when you are BIG?"*

Whether you need wholesale change or a tweak to your pattern, the power of the question will serve you well, "Who are you when you are BIG?" It's truly a state of mind by which you can gain perspective for progress. It's the state of empowerment, and you can step into it whenever you want. Even during the course of a single day, you can pull yourself out of the smallness you might feel when you are weary yet need to make a major presentation, for example.

> **The BIG mindset can be your game changer.**

The BIG mindset can be your game changer. The application can be for the long term, certainly, but it can be for the short term, as well. Practiced consistently, it becomes a way of life, a dedication to happiness. You can write down who you are when you are BIG and use it for daily inspiration. Let's say you are a mother living a hectic life of getting your children to school and back, shopping for groceries, fixing dinner, helping with homework, and activity after activity. You can choose to feel floored by it all. Or you can see yourself as living large in that role of motherhood, cherishing every moment with your children. And if, for a time, it doesn't seem that way, you can always choose to slip back into that BIG state of mind.

The pursuit of positivity

Many of us are taught to be problem solvers, especially as leaders in business. We focus on what's wrong and fixing problems and removing obstacles, and that's what has made a lot of leaders successful. What we find is that many people, so caught up in what they should or shouldn't be doing, fall victim to their inner voices of negativity. We have become so used to focusing on what is wrong or broken that we lose sight of what is right. We magnify our problems, but not our victories.

With our clients, we find that initially they may be trying to move away from an undesired state. They are focused on a problem and how to make it go away, whether it be just a lack of confidence, curing a weakness, fixing a relationship, or getting rid of their stress. We have them look instead to their desired state and envision what they want to move toward rather than what they are running from. For instance, what does more confidence look like or feel like? What will they have when the weakness is gone? What is the desired state of the relationship? What is their life like when they can control their stress? Our focus is on the desired outcome rather than on the problem.

When we tap into BIG, we're putting the magnifying glass on what may be some small aspect that we can grow and grow and grow. We give power to the positive.

What you focus on is what will grow.

Though we work primarily with business leaders, we have seen firsthand how the power of positivity can lift

> **What you focus on is what will grow.**

people in any of the domains of their lives—whether at work or at play, or in their finances, friendships, family, or romantic life. Leadership goes far beyond the corporate office. We ask our clients to think of all the roles in their lives, because each impacts the others. It's not just who they are as the boss. It's who they are as the peer or as a colleague. It's who they are as a parent, or as a son or daughter, or as a sibling. Who are they when they're BIG as a volunteer or as a coach of their kid's soccer team or in a nonprofit organization? Who are they when they are BIG as a friend?

When we nurture our yearnings, when we pursue the positive, our ideas can grow into possibilities and then into realities. If you grasp that, then you can do wonders for yourself, your business, your family, and your community. The yearning is in each of us. So many of us want fulfillment, to live a pleasant life with great purpose—to be BIG and when we find it, it ripples outward.

This book is for those who are at the pinnacle looking down, perhaps feeling overwhelmed, or who are at the bottom looking up. Whether you are a corporate leader or a household leader, or both, this book is for you. It is for the entrepreneur feeling his or her way in the business world. It's for those who are unemployed and searching, or troubled and feeling trapped. You show leadership in picking up the reins and moving forward, even in the face of turbulence.

How we saw the BIG picture

All journeys have a beginning. As we embark on this discovery of who you are when you are BIG, we will tell you our own stories, so that you can see that we each have been where you now may find yourself—that is, wondering what more life might hold if only we knew more about ourselves.

The "we" throughout most of this book is the common voice of Kimberly Roush and Allan Milham. Though our coaching practices are separate, we are united in philosophy. We have helped each other on our individual journeys, and we share beliefs about how people can reach the next level. Though we work primarily with executives, those principles apply to many people in the wide range of life's domains.

In our stories, included in Chapter 3 and Chapter 6, we will switch from our collective voice of "we" to our separate voices as "I." We each will step forward separately to explain who we are, where we have been, and where we are going as each of us pursues our own 'BIG.'

So, sit back, relax and enjoy the journey. You're in for something BIG!

BIG INSIGHTS:

- How ready am I to be liberated from the fear that holds me back or keeps me playing small?

- What do I yearn for that would have me being BIGger in life?

- What within me wants to emerge to give, provide, or offer to the world?

- How hungry am I to create a more purposeful and fulfilling life?

When I am BIG . . .

Who I am when I'm BIG or at the very top of my game?

I'm John Travolta strutting down the street to the beat of "Stayin' Alive," breathing pure rarefied air.

I'm Midas; everything I touch turns to gold.

I'm Doc Holiday; every decision I make is faster than his draw and more accurate than his aim.

I'm Steve Martin; as the pressure builds I crack jokes to help keep everyone around me relaxed.

I'm Superman; nothing can hurt me, nothing can touch me, and I'm impervious to pain.

Then "Jesus Christ Superstar" starts playing in my head and I hear a voice announce "United Flight 7419 boarding to Cincinnati." As I get off the plane, I'm greeted by my three best friends since forever and I know before the weekend's over I'll be a little country kid from Ohio again, not John Travolta, not Midas, not Doc Holiday, not Steve Martin, not Superman, not JC, and not even Rodney Dangerfield, as my best friends give me no respect but bring me back to earth. As the little country kid from Ohio boards the flight back to L.A., I hear in my mind, "Thank you for being a friend."

—**MICHAEL MCLEOD,**
Head of Sales, Dunvegan Enterprise

CHAPTER 2

It's not about
BIG ego

Sometimes when we talk about BIG, people immediately think we're talking about having a big ego. Let us be emphatically clear: BIG is not about ego or title or position or money. It's about who you are when you are engaged and energized and full of life. You are BIG when you are at your best, and when you are jazzed to get up and go to work each morning. You are BIG when you are in the flow, when everything feels right, and life and work seem effortless.

Ego is a funny thing, though. Rarely do we ourselves know when we have a big ego, although it is often easy to spot in others. We have found that big egos might

> **BIG is not about ego or title or position or money. It's about who you are when you are engaged and energized and full of life.**

be driving people who's sense of self-worth is tied to

what they have attained, how hard they work, the results they have achieved, or how much money they make. Sometimes, it's the car they drive or the house they live in. Sometimes, self-worth is tied to who is proud of them or what other people think. True self-worth doesn't depend on any of these things. Everyone, regardless of socioeconomic circumstance or education, has true self-worth—we are born with it. Some of the richest people in the world are those with very little material wealth.

The ego: The good, the bad, and the ugly

Big ego is defined as an overinflated sense of self worth. BIG is not talking about over-valuing but rather understanding and operating from your true value—based on those core values that ground you.

> **BIG is not talking about over-valuing but rather understanding and operating from your true value—based on those core values that ground you.**

Ego serves us in many ways. It allows us to believe in ourselves, and to move forward and to do the things we love. It was our egos that propelled both of us to success as coaches.

Even when their egos are flourishing, many people feel

strongly that they must come across as humble. You can sense a false modesty as people try to abide by what they feel is the cultural dictate to not act like a big shot. Further, people who are humble or those who have taken a hit to their ego must be careful that they don't translate that into a feeling of guilt if they aspire to great heights and wealth. They can come to believe that ego is inherently bad. In their desire to escape an unfulfilling career and pursue their passion, they could think of ego as a sham. They fear being led astray by ego.

Such an attitude actually can hold back people who are on a mission of change. It can inhibit their growth. They want so much to live for their passion that they think doing it for the money is somehow bad. It's important to understand that we can have a healthy ego.

If it wasn't for our egos, we wouldn't get up in the morning. We need and deserve to feel good about ourselves.

If it wasn't for our egos, we wouldn't get up in the morning. We need and deserve to feel good about ourselves. As coaches, we know. We relish the greatness inside of others, and we feel privileged that we get to watch it emerge.

Carly, a leader in a large retail organization, had a reputation for being one tough manager. She was proud of her
powerful results, but managed by fear and intimidation.
It was not that she was a mean woman, but she somehow
came to believe that to get results and move up the
ladder, she had to change personalities when she came
to work. People were intimidated, and many employees
left abruptly while working for her. As Carly says: "Hey,
my style is how I was managed, and it gets results." A
new division leader was hired two years ago and arrived
with a very different mindset, and it became clear that
Carly's style of managing would have to change.

Carly was so focused on getting things done quickly that
she really did not see the cost of her style. She had a very
short temper, operated at sixty miles an hour, and had no
patience for incompetence or "slow" people with lots of
questions. She expected that people would understand
their role after she explained what was required of them.
They agreed to her dictates, for fear that they would be
eliminated right out of the gate. After all, results were
all that really mattered and she was proud of what she
produced.

Through coaching, Carly came to realize she was a brash
move maker. She had been operating out of fear and
anxiety of not performing well, and with low self-esteem.
She overcompensated with unhealthy ego. Carly started

to notice her impact more and began to learn how to lead by increasing trust, letting go of control, and developing patience. Carly learned to shift her mindset so that she could be curious and ask questions, rather than controlling all situations and telling team members what to do. The behavior change surprised many around her. One employee wondered if she had received bad health news!

Over the coming months, Carly learned to adopt Stephen Covey's principle, "Seek first to understand—then be understood." She consciously began meetings with open-ended questions starting with "what" or "how." The results were dramatic. Peers and direct reports began to refer to Carly as "CC," for Curiosity Carly, which she actually appreciated. She was amazed at how collaboration was increasing, as she got out of the way by loosening up with her directive "always-must-have-the-answer" style. She became an inquisitive learner, inviting the team members to be a part of the solutions.

Team members felt more empowered by this new leadership style, and she discovered that she did not have to micromanage to get things done. They were getting greater results, and people enjoyed coming to work. She even negotiated a union contract, and colleagues were stunned at how she masterfully collaborated.

She soon realized that the previous way she had learned

to manage had taken a huge toll. She had not liked being the tough manager with the heavy hand. She began getting great performance evaluations and found people enjoyed being around her. The ego that once made enemies now made allies.

Carly began playing BIG and was able to lead from a place of authenticity and transparency. She found greater happiness in her work; her doctor was pleased that her blood pressure was lower; and her boss, who earlier had put her on the transition list, was now one of her greatest cheerleaders.

Three levels of listening

Big ego is a funny thing. It lives in our heads, and the way to a healthy ego comes down to this: Listen up!

At CTI, coaches in training learn about three levels of listening. In the book *Co-Active Coaching*, the authors describe the three levels of listening:

Level I: Internal Listening

At Level I, our attention is on *ourselves*. We listen to the words of the other person, but the focus is on what it means to us. At Level I, the spotlight is on me: my thoughts, my judgments, my feelings, and my conclusions about myself and others. Whatever is happening with the other person is coming back to me through a diode: a one-way energy trap that lets information in but not out. I'm absorbing information by listening, but holding it in a trap that recycles it. At Level I, there is only one question: What does this mean to me? There are many times when this is entirely appropriate; for instance, when you are traveling alone to a different city, you are likely to be operating at Level I most of the time. All of your attention is on yourself, as it should be.

Level II: Focused Listening

At Level II, there is a sharp focus on the *other person*. You can see it in people's posture when they are communicating at Level II: probably both leaning forward, looking intently at each other. There is a great deal of attention on the other person and not much awareness of the outside world.

Level III: Global Listening

At Level III, you listen at 360 degrees. In fact, you listen as though you and the other person were at the center of the universe, receiving information from everywhere at once. It's as though you're surrounded by a force field that contains you, the other person, and a space of knowing. Level III includes everything you can observe with your senses: what you see, hear, smell, and feel—the tactile sensations as well as the emotional sensations. Level III includes the action, the inaction, and the interaction.

Imagine yourself in a meeting where you were more focused on the voices inside your own head than to what the other participants were saying. Perhaps you were thinking of what you were going to say next, or that you didn't agree with the person speaking. Maybe you were thinking about your kid's soccer game or all the things you needed to get done. When you are in your own head, you may think you are listening, but you are really only listening to yourself. Now, imagine yourself engrossed in conversation or listening intently to a speaker (Level II). Imagine yourself in a meeting where you were keenly aware that there was confusion or that a break was necessary (Level III).

> **When you are BIG, your ego doesn't control you. It's healthy ego.**

When you are BIG, your ego doesn't control you. It's healthy ego. When we operate from a healthy ego, Level II and Level III listening are much easier. No longer is it all about "me, me, me." Great leaders know it is about their followers.

Henry Kimsey-House, co-founder of CTI, goes on to

describe Leadership as Level IV below. The following is an excerpt from an interview with Henry:

> *What might surprise people who know about how we talk about level I, II, III listening and awareness, in our coaching programs, is that for us leadership is Level IV. The leader sets that stake very clearly in place, and Level IV is the action that happens around it. It starts with an urge, within the powerful Level I self of a leader, then marries itself with the urge coming from the Level III, the space or field surrounding us. We assert that the Level III actually has needs and the leader's job is to marry their urge or need with the urge or need of the space around them. I+III=IV. And as you begin to find a way to match those two urges, what happens is a compelling need to act emerges, and that's where the leader then gets into action."*

From "me" to "we"

Later in this book, we will discuss the concept of leading yourself first. Much of leading yourself comes from emotional intelligence—self-awareness and self-management. Tapping into "who you are when you are BIG" is a valuable tool to help you lead yourself first—not from a place of ego, but from a place of empowerment.

Leaders who are BIG are authentic. They are true to their inner values and core beliefs. They are not driven by outside influences (power, fame, status, ego, etc.), but rather by inner forces that provide strength. This strength is the pillar of BIG leadership. With this strength, we can come from a place of learning and curiosity, allow vulnerability, and rise together. The focus no longer needs to be on the "me," it can be on the "we."

It's in this mode that we can lead from what the Level III space is calling for. The higher levels of emotional intelligence focus on social awareness and relationship management. With social awareness, you can assess a situation as if you were not part of it, almost as if you were looking down and observing what was happening. From there, you can more readily see what is needed in each relationship and in the situation. Level IV leadership encompasses all levels of emotional intelligence. When you are BIG in leading yourself first, you invite others to be BIG, too, and the leadership of "we" emerges.

Ego of the heart

A healthy ego opens a sense of curiosity about what it means to be BIG. When we come from an unstable or unhealthy ego, as Carly learned, it comes at quite a cost.

Healthy ego comes when you feel proud of who you are

inside. You feel BIG, in that you have come to understand what makes you thrive. Your ego doesn't feed on the thought, "I'm bigger than you." It thrives on the thought, "I'm BIG because I've made the best of myself, and I know you can do the same." BIG is not the ego of a big head. It's the ego of a BIG heart.

> **BIG is not the ego of a big head. It's the ego of a BIG heart.**

That's when you are BIG. Your ego has the right outlook—it is healthy, and it motivates you to do your best for yourself, your family, and your community. You are in a special zone, and it is an empowered and peaceful place, a soothing state of mind. Life has gotten a whole lot easier.

BIG INSIGHTS:

1. **What would be possible if I shifted from "me" to "we" in my leadership?**

2. **How does my humility keep me playing small?**

3. **What is the ego of my heart saying?**

When I am BIG . . .

Who I Am When I Am BIG . . . Captain of Work and Life!

As polished as a fine vessel entering the harbor under full sail
A little older, weathered and experienced but still bristol
Wisdom to realize that youth and inexperience still has a voice

Brave to leave port as nothing was ever explored without leaving
the harbor
Confidence that there are times to use a drogue in the face of
a gale
Wisdom to always remember that my family (wife and son) are my
anchor

Smart as a tactician plotting a lay line to the final mark
Strong as a grinder turning his winch using hard work to win
the race
Wisdom to know that ALL positions are required for the TEAM
to win

My compass rose steers straight, personally and professionally
Discipline although never pleasant will always be necessary
Wisdom to know when it's time to "walk the plank" or "swab
the deck"

As accurate as a sextant to stay on course while using my log to
learn from history
Intelligent enough to know they are only tools and will never
replace common sense
Wisdom to know that the stars will guide but remembering to see
the beauty in the heavens

That in time of trials, the waves and challenges may be larger
than life
There will be times to use autopilot or times for the hands-on
touch of experience
Wisdom to remember "In God I Trust" for help to know when to
use which

Laughter will always keep your crew alert and the task seem small
Humor or daily portions of grog are great to keep the crew
together and having fun
Wisdom to raise my family with laughter as a cornerstone and
never take myself too seriously

Remember that we only live once with my family as priority
Fair Winds and Fair Friends is more than a toast
Wisdom to ALWAYS—Live my life as a Journey NOT a guided tour!

—KEN DONKERSLOOT
Software Development Executive,
Genesis Consulting

CHAPTER 3

Kimberly's story: Out of my head and into my heart

I remember the swirl of three straight years full of consistent sixty-hour workweeks, particularly early in my career. I once mentioned to my father how much overtime I was putting in, and he responded: "Good, good, good!" I let him in on how I was feeling: "No, Dad, it's not good."

My career began in public accounting, which is a demanding profession where sixty- and even eighty-hour workweeks are not uncommon. If you hope to be successful, you jump whenever the client calls. I pretty much was a workaholic. The harder I worked, the more successful I was becoming—or at least that's what I thought. I learned early on, and it was ingrained in me, that you had to take initiative for your own career. If you wanted to move up, you had to let people know what you wanted. You had to make sure you got the training you needed and to make sure that you had the necessary sponsorship or support or mentorship. You had to be in charge of that and not expect anybody to do it for you.

Fifteen years later, my job as Regional Professional Practice Partner at KPMG. LLP (KPMG or "the firm") entailed approving every new client and every new contract for 34 partners in the western area. In other words, I stood in the way of revenue. If those 34 partners didn't do what was necessary for me to approve their contracts, they didn't point the finger at themselves. They were upset with me. The stress was intense, and in addition to this role, I also was responsible for overseeing Information Technology (IT) support in financial statement audits for most of southern California during the implementation of the Sarbanes-Oxley Act. Both were intense full-time jobs.

The Professional Practice Partner role was a major ego boost. It was a position specially approved for me by the firm's Risk Management Committee, since I had been a partner less than the required five years. But playing those two roles meant that I now was working more than 80 hours a week. I was having a hard time keeping up. After a time, the firm asked that I just do the IT audit support, citing increased focus needed on the new regulations in the profession. It was a huge blow to my ego.

Meanwhile, another element of my career was shining

brightly. I was receiving the Chairman's Award for Excellence in Volunteerism. It was a prestigious honor, recognizing work I had been doing for several years with the firm team I created for a 100-mile Multiple Sclerosis (MS) bike ride. I had gotten MS recognized as a fourth national charity for the firm, meaning each office in the nation participates in an annual event for MS.

Still, I was discouraged over the loss of my Professional Practice Partner role. I met over lunch with my mentor within the firm while I was in New York receiving the Chairman's Award. "I'm kind of thinking I should leave the firm," I told him. "I'm pretty discouraged." During that lunch, he offered me a role as national partner whose duty, in essence, would be to make sure the IT auditors and the financial statement auditors played nice together.

Some within the firm doubted I would be good at the job—"that's not her core strength," they said. I felt very unsure of myself going into this high-exposure national role. I'd had a lot of major roles, but this one intimidated me, particularly since I hadn't exactly received a vote of confidence.

I had to work up the courage to ask my boss if I could have an executive coach. At the time, my fear was the perception that coaches were for people who were broken and needed to be fixed, and that people would think of me as weak. I didn't feel weak asking for it, however. I knew it would be a powerful source of the support I wanted so much. As you move up within the firm, by the time you become a partner, there's nobody necessarily mentoring or guiding you anymore. You're a partner, and you're expected to know it all—or at least that's what I thought.

By then, I had already spoken to Allan, and I finally rallied the courage to ask my boss if I could hire and work with him. "Sure, that's a wonderful idea," he replied—far easier than I had anticipated. So began my coaching relationship with Allan. I needed his help in figuring out the best way to move forward in this new role. To get these two groups to play nicely together, I needed to influence two major leaders, the heads of the firm's Advisory and Audit Practices—and it could take me months to get on their calendars for fifteen minutes. I didn't feel like a leader among the leaders of the firm. I knew how to manage up and I knew how to communicate up, but influencing up was a new ball game for me.

So I asked Allan to help me work with leadership and influence primarily. I was telling myself things, such as, "I don't think like them," and "I'm not in their league." Allan requested that I work through an exercise, which we speak more about in Chapter 5 that led me to a new perspective. I replaced that limiting belief with the powerful assumption, "Of, course, you don't think like them—that's why they created this position for you. They need someone to solve this problem. It's mega-important, and you have something to offer."

It was the same statement: "I don't think like them." But it was an entirely different viewpoint. I switched from a feeling of "I don't belong" to one of "I bring a unique value." My state of weakness transformed to a state of strength. It made all the difference in the world in my state of mind when I walked into a conference room with these colleagues.

Three months into my new role, the chairman of our firm, Gene O'Kelly, was diagnosed with brain cancer and three months later he died. The firm was reorganizing.

"What's going on with your position?" Allan asked me.

"Oh, I'm safe. I'll be in this role for at least another year, and when I'm done with this, they'll give me some other great position, more title, more money, they always have, they always will."

"Wow," he said, then added, "Kimberly, what would it be like for you to consider the part of your job that you love, that you're really great at, the part that energizes you and gets you out of bed each day, and then figure out the role within KPMG that would allow you to do that the most? Suppose you were to spend this next year positioning yourself for that job—what would that be like?"

It was what we call one of those "a-ha!" moments. What were those words that had just come out of my mouth? Had I really said, "Oh, they'll just give me some other great position"? Since when had I handed over responsibility for the progression of my career—and my happiness, for that matter—to somebody else? How passive was that?

As I pondered that question, I got to thinking. I recalled a time early in my career when I was assigned an audit that nobody in the office wanted to work on. The relationship with the client was pretty bad, and it was an important account. The managing partner pulled me into his office and said, "We *chose you* because we think *you're* the one who can turn this around."

From that point on, I took numerous positions that nobody else in the firm wanted. It fed my ego. I did that time and again. The whole reason I got that Professional Practice Partner role early is because nobody else wanted it. The reason I was doing the IT audit support was because nobody else wanted to do it.

I always did those jobs with great pride, and I was proud of my contributions in turning those situations around, but my success had a lot to do with coaching and mentoring and challenging and inspiring others. I did that every day—and yet it was not primarily what I was getting paid to do. It was sort of a sideline, an ancillary part of my job. Still, public accounting gives you so much opportunity to work that way with others, and that's what kept me in that business all those years.

"What if you got to choose?" Allan said to me. "What if you were the one driving?" Our generation had been taught to put our heads down, work hard, do what we were asked, never say no, and great things will happen. For the most part, great things had happened for me,

> **"What if you got to choose?" Allan said to me.**

but I realized that I had not been in the driver's seat in a lot of respects.

I had sought out and wanted every one of those positions along the way, but largely I wanted them because they fed my ego, not because they fed my happiness. So much of my job in my later years was frustrating and stressful. While I was in those dual roles, before working with Allan, I had become obese. During one busy season, I got sick four times and was on my fifth round of antibiotics in four months. During one particularly bad round of bronchitis and sinusitis after an hour-long conference call, I would need three hours on the couch just to recover.

I realized I needed to manage the stress, so I started working with a personal trainer. That's when I realized I was 40 pounds overweight and 40 percent body fat. I had just figured my husband took bad pictures! I lost those pounds in six months and learned about all sorts of things I hadn't known I could do. I learned there were trails right outside my house. I started enjoying sunrises and sunsets—and friendships. I began running and competing in half-marathons, marathons, and mini-triathlons. I was in a whole different place. And it was my trainer who referred me to Allan. That was in 2005, and I continue working with Allan to this day.

Again, my original goal was to deal with issues of leadership and influence, but Allan kept asking me to consider what motivated me the most—the best reasons for getting up in the morning and staying late at work. This continued for several months.

One night, I found myself still at the office at 11 p.m.—and I was having fun. I was recruiting people for the MS bike ride at all levels in the firm. I was presenting people with a big challenge, and I believed in them to succeed.

I loved the camaraderie. It was fun.

Why was this so meaningful to me? I thought of the look on people's faces in Mission Bay Park in San Diego after they had ridden a hundred miles in two days. Two months earlier, some hadn't even owned a bike. They had accomplished something that had been beyond their wildest dreams. I realized how much I loved this part of my job.

> **The question to ask is this: When does the work feel like play? Where does it seem effortless, with no hint of drudgery?**

"Maybe," I thought, "this is what Allan has been trying to get me to see." People sometimes spend years—an entire career, perhaps—without getting in touch with their core strengths and passions. I had gone decades. The question to ask is this: When does the work feel like play? Where does it seem effortless, with no hint of drudgery?

We continued to examine what really resonated with me, what I loved about my job. Until then, I had focused on those things that I was known for being good at doing. For my next position, I had always aimed for a more prestigious step in the same direction that I'd been taking. To help me evaluate the possibilities, Allan had me develop a list of my strengths and my weaknesses, my likes and my dislikes, my values. I looked down that column, and I realized everything that I had written involved people—coaching, developing, mentoring, challenging, and inspiring people.

I pictured myself in a new career—doing the same thing for others that Allan had done for me. But how could I even mention that to him? He was a Master Certified Coach, at the top of his game. I felt small by comparison. In our next coaching session, however, I broached the prospect.

"So what about coaching?" I asked him, and quickly added: "But who am I to think I can do what you do?"

"Who are you to think you can't?" he asked back.

"What do you mean?"

"You've been coaching people for 22 years," he said. "It's the part of your job you love. It's why you get out of bed every morning."

"Well, yeah, but . . ." We take our strengths for granted—they come so easily to us that we often don't place a value on them.

"You've been working with CEOs and CIOs and CFOs and boards of directors and audit committees for how many years? You can walk right into the field of executive coaching if you desire," Allan said.

I felt incredulous. I would have thought that such a dramatic career change from public accounting would require me to start at the

> **We take our strengths for granted—they come so easily to us that we often don't place a value on them.**

bottom and work my way up. But he was suggesting to me I could just launch into the top five percent of the coaching profession.

In our coaching sessions, I realized that I had a unique skillset, given my business skills, passion for coaching and mentoring, and experience at the executive level.

I thought, "He just wrote my business plan." It still took me several months to take that partner hat off my head. But how cool would it be, I realized, to spend 100 percent of my time every day doing what I love, and none of the stuff I don't love. So, I made this Bold Move just as Allan was publishing his book.

It was bold, but it wasn't a brash move. I didn't just up and decide to quit one day. I started to take coaching classes in January 2007. I had been through four of the five core classes at CTI and in April of that year approached the firm about leaving, doing so in November 2007. I was off to this incredibly exciting time in my life.

My ego had been pretty big in public accounting, and I'll be the first to admit that now in hindsight. Quite frankly, I think that a lot of ego is involved in running corporate America. Egos drive many people in high-level positions. I left a national position as a partner in a global firm. I'd been with the best of the best in public accounting.

Then one day I left to become an entrepreneur. No more resources at my fingertips. I had to buy my own photocopier and make my own photocopies. That was the day I became Kimberly Roush.

And I felt small. I told Allan about it.

"Excuse me," he said, "but did you leave any part of your accomplishments at KPMG?"

"No."

"Did you leave any part of Kimberly Roush there? Her experience, her personality?"

"No."

"So tell me, who is Kimberly Roush when she is BIG?"
It wasn't about ego, or title, or money. It was about who
I was when I was on my game and jazzed to get up and
go to work in the morning. He gave me an assignment:
write out my answer. I did. In November 2007, this was
my perception of who I was when I was BIG:

*When I am BIG, I'm confident, I'm happy, I'm
smiling, singing, doing the "I got it going on" dance.*

*I'm busy. I'm sought after. I'm a keynote speaker and
author. I don't have time to procrastinate. I don't
have time to question myself. I'm proud of myself.
My husband, family, and friends are proud of me.*

*I love my work, I love my clients, I love getting
up for work in the morning. I'm helping others, I
love myself, I am giving, I am not concerned about
making it.*

*I'm personable, approachable, outgoing, conversa-
tional, a good listener; I'm energetic and enthusiastic. I have a passion and a vision. I'm on purpose.
I am focused. I am healthy. I exercise regularly and
I'm at my ideal weight.*

It had been hard to part with my self-image from my career in public accounting. I felt as if I were packing away a trophy I had pursued for 22 years. That career had defined so much of me, and to step out and do something else was frankly intimidating. But in all those years, I hadn't really put a value on the true strengths that I brought to my career. I was beginning to see that I could make a living doing just the fun part of my job.

As I started my business, I was introduced to Christi Haley Stover of Platinum Resource Group. We were both networking like crazy and meeting hundreds of executives in transition. We couldn't help but notice how much we felt like those executives in transition as we were starting our own businesses. We began helping them one by one and realized there was so much they could do to help each other and "Boot Camp for Executives In Transition" was born. Shortly thereafter, Tenny Poole of Positive Talents Strategies joined forces with us as a sponsor and co-facilitator.

We have used the BIG concept in our boot camps with executives—more than 900 of them so far, as we write this book. To each new group that comes in monthly, we emphasize that coaching and boot camp is not for people who are broken and need to be fixed. Rather, it is for people who are stuck and want to be empowered, or who just want more in their lives, or want to aspire to the greatness that is already within them.

We have helped them boost their self-esteem, tap into where they have thrived in their careers, and identify what might be getting in the way of their greatness. For the fourth week of every boot camp, we ask them to write an answer to the question, "Who are you when you are BIG?" We then ask them to be BIG when they read it to the group. Their eyes sparkle. They are in the room with 13 other people who also feel good about themselves again. Collectively, the whole room gets BIGger!

My witnessing of those BIG boot camp experiences was an inspiration for this book. I have seen nearly one thousand "When I am BIG" writings submitted by participants and clients. You've seen some of them in chapters of this book. As I have observed how the boot campers' lives and careers and outlook have improved, and as I have seen their power emerge, it has become clear to me that the message needs a broader audience. We must make this even BIGGER.

As I tell my story and reflect on my own evolution of attitude, I particularly recall those four powerful questions that Allan posed to me over the course of just a year or two. Let me repeat them, this time posing them to you:

BIG INSIGHTS

- What aspects of my work have me energized and engaged?

- What if I could do just what I love to do?

- Who am I to think I can't?

- And perhaps most powerful of all, "Who am I when I am BIG?"

When I am BIG . . .

As a coach
I challenge, inspire
I listen and I am curious
I am compassionate and empathetic
I don't fix, because nobody is broken. I don't help, because nobody is helpless. I serve.
I believe in the greatness inside of people and acknowledge their humanity
I relish every moment of what I am doing
I collaborate with those who are equally passionate about their life's work.
I hold my clients BIG.
I have the privilege of getting to witness magnificence emerge.

As a wife
I express my love to my husband every day in ways that make him feel loved, appreciated, and acknowledged.
I thank him for my coffee every morning, my clean laundry every week, the groceries he retrieves, the home he has provided and keeps up, the sleep I get when he gets up with the dogs, the love and care he gives, the support he provides in my activities and my business, the grill master that he is, the attention he provides to my family, the stabilizing force he is in my life and, for sure, his sense of humor.
I melt in the security of his embrace.
I listen for what is magnificent in his world.
I remember my sexy side.

As an athlete
I honor my body and respect it for the amazing system that it is.
I fuel my body with rich nutrients and not junk, even when I've
    earned the extra calories.
I find ways to choose activity instead of sedimentary options.
I create good stress for my body and blast away bad stress.
I challenge myself to break barriers—every time I do, it is a
    metaphor for my life.
I care for my body when it says it needs it.
I take pride in a good workout that leaves my lungs full of fresh
    air, has allowed sweat to flush my body of impurities, has
    filled my body with endorphins that put a spring in my step
    throughout the day, and fills my mind with the can-do-ed-ness
    and confidence no money can buy.

As a person
My heart is filled with joy.
I am playful. I laugh often; I smile big.
I live in positivity.
I'm not working at anything, but rather playing with everything.
I am energetic and enthusiastic.
I operate from my strengths.
My ego is in check and I am vulnerable.
I give more energy than I take even when I could use a little love.

—KIMBERLY ROUSH

CHAPTER 4

BIG is easy

I
n Greek mythology, Sisyphus faces an eternal pun-
ishment in which he must repeatedly push a huge
stone up a hill every day, only to see it roll back
down every night. The gods have condemned Sisyphus
for his deceitfulness, and his ultimate torment is hopeless
and pointless labor.

We mortals often submit to such drudgery in life, and
we deceive ourselves when we do. There's no reason to
live that way. It is as if many of us metaphorically step
into playing Sisyphus each morning and strain to push
that boulder. We push and push, and when we finally
get into bed, we count it a victory. We survived another
day, and come the morrow we will do it again.

As executive coaches, we have seen this so many times.
A client is feeling worn out from the stress of the daily
push. Our advice: Stop pushing, and start playing.
Think of yourself as jaunting to the top of the hill and
then using your natural savvy and ingenuity to devise
a pulley system that does the job with a fraction of the

effort. The work becomes fun, as you relish your creative powers. You are just doing what comes naturally. And if that heavy weight does start to slip, you will be on the upside. You can let go without getting creamed.

What you get to do

Our coaching includes work with leaders who are business owners who can sometimes feel overwhelmed. It can be daunting being the top person in charge and having all the responsibility fall on them. They might say to themselves, "I have too much to do—I can't keep up. I need to be responsible for all these employees. I have to worry about making payroll. I feel like I should work all the time—I never get a break. I have to be strong—no one can see me sweat. I have to bring in all the sales."

Suppose they shift their perspective and instead say this: "Thank goodness I have so much to do—I 'get to' keep building my business. I 'get to' be responsible for all these employees—look what I am getting to provide them. I'm fortunate enough to 'get to' pay people for their service. I'm the boss—I 'get to' work when I want—I 'get to' give myself a break. I 'get to' be a strong leader for my employees—how can I inspire them? I 'get to' continue actively interacting with customers—it keeps me close to the market."

Being a business owner becomes a privilege. It's no longer a matter of I "have to," "need to," "ought to," or "should." What if they thought about it like that every day? What if you did? Life becomes magical.

Defining your "optimal operating state"

Today we have so many tools and resources to help us reflect and assess who we are—to uncover our gifts and talents, our values and beliefs. They are all inside us, waiting to be activated. It's as if we have an operating manual for living, but unfortunately, sometimes we lose that manual.

> **It's as if we have an operating manual for living, but unfortunately, sometimes we lose that manual.**

We can always return to the central question, however. In a tech-filled world, we might put it like this: What is your Optimal Operating State? What do you need so that you do not feel vulnerable, or depleted, or flat-lined?

If you are feeling that way, you are in the "barely move" state of the barely-brash-bold continuum that we described. You're barely getting by. You are breathing, yes, but you are really unplugged and you are not putting a lot of energy into the quality of your life. You are in the "brash move" state when fear and doubt set in, and your thinking is dominated by scarcity. To be in the Bold Move state, you need to keep track of that manual. When you operate optimally, you can do more than you might have imagined.

So what does that look like to you? We are all unique and different, so what does it mean for you to be in an optimal operating state? If you can define it, you have a better chance to recover when you get thrown off, and we all get thrown off. We all get triggered. We all have our down moments. The trick is to recycle ourselves as quickly as possible. But you have to know how. You have to be equipped. And you have to take personal responsibility for staying on track—or, as we like to say, once you recognize who you really are, you get to "own" it.

When a client begins to receive coaching, the goal isn't to expect an immediate "a-ha!" of self-discovery. Rather, in our practices, we take stock and inventory of what is unique and remarkable about our clients and how that translates into leadership. When you take ownership of those traits, you are on the way to a more compelling life. You will be all the more powerful as a leader, not just in your career but at home and in the community, and being BIG will come easily.

What makes it easy and fun?

So how is this relevant? Is there enough meat in this advice to actually help a client? When we talk about ease and effortlessness, some people insist, "No! Work is hard, and you have to put a lot of effort into it." We're not saying that taking it easy puts you in touch with the real you. We're saying that when you are the real you—when you are BIG—it's easy.

Has there been a time in your life when things just seemed easy? What were the circumstances? What allowed it to be easy? Maybe it was the people you were working with, or maybe it was your relationship with them. If you are struggling with something, ask yourself this: What would make it easy? You might be surprised to find that you can come up with an answer right on the spot.

> *We're not saying that taking it easy puts you in touch with the real you. We're saying that when you are the real you—when you are BIG—it's easy.*

Perhaps you just need someone to run your ideas past. If you come from corporate America, as most of our clients do, you likely can think of any number of people you could consult. You probably could walk down the hall and tap on most any office door. When you are no longer alone in trying to push that stone, the hill becomes less imposing. Even if others do not sweat alongside you, they can offer perspectives for a better way.

And it's all from that question, "What would make it easy?" We have a choice. We can look at our challenges as insurmountable, and that's what they will become. Or we can assume there are solutions out there for us to find—and they will come to us. If we cease the pointless labor and start playing with ideas, we will have them in abundance. Yes, work takes effort. But it need not be onerous. The effort can be so much fun that it seems to be no work at all.

> **We make a choice every day as to whether we are going to play small or step into being BIG. Small comes from fear and doubt. BIG comes from hope and possibility.**

So the question really amounts to this: Are we addicted to drudgery or do we want to have fun? Maybe if we find ourselves having fun we will get a lot more done, and it may bring even greater financial rewards, as well. It's when you are doing what is meaningful to you that you will find it easy. It's when you are motivated from within, not from without. As coaches, we care about clients' career accomplishments, but we care even more about what they truly find meaningful and enjoy doing—what comes so easy to them that it is effortless. When we hear about that—when their eyes sparkle—they are telling us their core strengths, beliefs, and values. We are hearing the essence of what gets them charged up. We hear what they want to amplify in their lives.

It's all about states of mind

It's a mental game. What will keep you in a positive frame of mind? Marathon runners know that their greatest obstacle is their own mind. If you can put that in a place of positivity, there's no stopping you. Once you know who you are when you are BIG, it is a state of mind you can step into at any moment. We make a choice

> **"Whether you think you can, or think you can't," it is often said, "you're right."**

every day as to whether we are going to play small or step into being BIG. Small comes from fear and doubt. BIG comes from hope and possibility.

"Whether you think you can, or think you can't," it is often said, "you're right." If you tell yourself, "I can do it," then you can. If you ask yourself how you will ever get through this, you won't. We all know from experience how much more energy we have in an atmosphere of positivity. Negative people will drag you down if you let them. You don't have to let them. That's a lesson for life.

We must go for what we yearn for. We ask clients where in life they are not taking ownership of that yearning. Is it in their career? Their family relationships? Are they living up to their standards for fitness and health? How about getting their finances in order? We love the expression, "Hope is not a strategy." Yearning without a plan or any action is playing small. It's an unresourceful state of mind.

Hope is not a strategy.

Perhaps you yearn for a better balance between work and the rest of your life—you want that work/life balance that has become a catchphrase at so many companies. Trying to address employee demand, companies offer childcare and elder care and sick childcare and concierge services. The goal is to take care of the extraneous worries and concerns that can drag down an employee so that performance suffers. But the key is to not wait for your company or anyone to do that for you. If you step into being BIG, you can be creative, resourceful, and take control. Start with small things that can have a BIG impact. What two small things would make you feel like you had work/life balance this week and how could you make those happen? There's hope. There's possibility. It all starts with changing your state of mind.

First, you must recognize your heart's desire—or else how could you go for it? We all need to deeply reflect on our inner lives and move toward those things that we find meaningful.

> **First, you must recognize your heart's desire—or else how could you go for it?**

Playing to your strengths

A Gallup survey asked a thousand people to respond to this statement: "At work, I have the opportunity to do what I do best every day." As you might expect, none of those who disagreed or strongly disagreed were emotionally engaged in their jobs. Those who agreed were six times more likely to be engaged in their jobs, and they were three times more likely to report that their quality of life in general was excellent.

We find job satisfaction when we play to our strengths. Doing so promotes excellence, success, productivity, and performance. Things come easily. We feel a sense of joy, flow, energy, and fulfillment. Each of us has strengths that are unique and enduring, and it is in our strengths that we have the greatest room for growth. A strength is a combination of talent, knowledge, and skills—things that come naturally, facts and lessons we learn, abilities we develop as we take the right steps.

> **People often focus instead on their weaknesses— and that's no fun.**

People often focus instead on their weaknesses—and that's no fun. We're always trying to fix what's wrong. Feeling deficient, we try to close the gap. We end up acting defensively, blaming, pointing a finger. Our inner critic shouts into our ears through a megaphone.

By contrast, focusing on our strengths is fun and fulfilling. We're celebrating what is right. We're feeling engaged, we're reaching for possibilities, and we're collaborating and engaged in teamwork.

In our work, we know that our clients have access to a positive inner voice that is encouraging them and giving them strength and telling them to rock on. In the book *Bold Moves*, this voice is referred to as "the Whisperer." We encourage clients to come up with their own name for this voice and "play with" magnifying it, so they can maintain a resourceful state of mind.

Positive psychology movement

Since the turn of the century, in our new millennium, positive psychology has gained further credibility as it has developed into a science and evidence-based movement, and that's likely to continue.

> **Focusing on our strengths is fun and fulfilling. We're celebrating what is right.**

Martin Seligman emphasized positive psychology during his term as president of the American Psychological Association. Instead of looking at mental disease and at what is wrong, he said, why not look at what it means to have a fulfilling, meaningful, pleasant life? He saw at the time that there were 45,000 studies on negative emotions—depression, anxiety, fear, phobias, and the like—compared with 300 related to the positive emotions. His conclusion: We're missing the boat. It's not the absence of disease that makes us healthy, he said, but rather our ability to cultivate the positive side.

The research and findings of the positive psychology movement support our principle of defining who you are when you are BIG and waking up consistently to breathe it, live it, believe it, and build on it.

The movement focuses on the very mindset that we are

advocating when we advise our clients to get in touch with their inner yearnings. As mentioned, researchers have learned that we can train ourselves to be more optimistic. They have designed exercises to help shift your mindset—sort of like going to a mental gym. For example, at bedtime every night, you could think of three things about the day for which you are grateful. Researchers have found that doing that consistently will create a new groove in your brain so that you wake up feeling more gratitude, and that positive orientation lingers throughout the day. A variety of research supports the neuroplasticity of our brains. We can reprogram ourselves.

A peer of Seligman's, Barbara Fredrickson, Ph.D., has been conducting research in this area for a decade, focusing on a positive vs. a negative orientation. She wrote a book called *Positivity*. As Dr. Fredrickson states, "with positivity, you see new possibilities, bounce back from setbacks, connect with others, and become the best version of yourself. You even sleep better." She has dedicated her career to examining positivity in people's emotional lives.

A psychologist by training, Dr. Fredrickson studied the effects of positive emotions on the brain, and won the Templeton Award for her work on the Broaden and Build Theory. She showed people central images that evoked either a positive emotion or a negative emotion. Each image also had peripheral images. Only the people shown pictures inducing positive emotions could see the peripheral images.

She found that negative images induced a state of negative emotions that evoked the fight or flight response—the instinct that we needed to run away from saber-toothed tigers. Fight-or-flight sends all our bodily resources to our major muscle groups to run fast, rather than to our brains. It also tends to shut down the immune system, and in our increasingly stressful lives, it may actually be the cause of some of the autoimmune disease spikes that we're seeing. When we are in a state of positive emotions, we are more creative and resourceful.

> *We're living in a world in which fear and doubt are on the rise. When we're in this state of negative emotions, we're not very connected to other people.*

We're living in a world in which fear and doubt are on the rise. When we're in this state of negative emotions, we're not very connected to other people. It's as if we are saying: "I'm looking out for me and I don't care about my neighbor because if I can run faster than him, he's lunch and I'm not." Further, according to Dr. Fredrickson's research, people in a negative state of emotions can't connect the dots, because they cannot see the dots (peripheral images). That's part of the reason we see our otherwise-resourceful clients finding themselves stuck. When we're in the state of positive emotions, our bodily resources can feed our brain, and open us to a mood of hope and possibility. It is in this state that accessing our BIG comes with ease and creates an upward spiral of positivity.

> **Scientific inquiry is finding hard facts around positivity, not soft fluff.**

Dr. Fredrickson's research also developed what she calls the Positivity Ratio, which is the proportion of positive to negative thoughts. When we're in a ratio of three positive thoughts to one negative one, we are thriving; when we are in a one-to-one ratio, we are depressed, or on the verge of depression.

The way you think about things greatly influences what you can accomplish and the opportunities you will encounter. The field of positive psychology focuses on building the best things in life rather than repairing the worst. The fact that positive psychology is now even more evidence based gives it added authority. There is research backing the power of positivity. From her research, Dr. Fredrickson offers the following facts to cement her case on positivity:

- **Fact 1—Positivity feels good**
- **Fact 2—Positivity changes how your mind works**
- **Fact 3—Positivity transforms your future**
- **Fact 4—Positivity puts the breaks on negativity**
- **Fact 5—Positivity obeys a tipping point (i.e., the sweet spot in between where a small change starts making a big difference)**
- **Fact 6—You can increase your positivity**

It's far more than just words. Scientific inquiry is finding hard facts around positivity, not soft fluff.

Rallying your resources

Management theorist Peter Drucker said, "The task of leadership is to align strengths in such a way that weaknesses are irrelevant." A Gallup study found that people stepping into successful leadership roles, in an organization or anywhere in their lives, were always investing in their strengths. These leaders surrounded themselves with the right people, who maximized their team and brought different strengths to the table. They understood their followers' needs, and they didn't imitate other leaders. Instead, they were true to themselves and capitalized on their own strengths.

Playing to your strengths has other benefits: Gallup found that people with low self-confidence reported three times as many health problems twenty-five years later. Those people with high self-evaluations actually reported fewer health problems in the same period. If you are aware of your strengths and build self-confidence while young, you can reap a cumulative advantage that continues to grow during your lifetime.

There are no unresourceful people, but there are unresourceful states of mind. What are those unresourceful states? They are the products of negativity. They include fear, doubt, and stress. People are often unresourceful when they feel overwhelmed, or when they become judgmental. Resourceful states are the positive ones: You are confident, empathetic, playful, energetic, enthusiastic, curious, joyful, loving, engaged, and grateful. Life, again, feels effortless.

When we're playing to our strengths with such a sense of ease, we are in the appropriate state that allows us to break through to our BIGness.

BIG INSIGHTS:

- In what aspects of my life am I pushing huge stones uphill?

- What would make it easier?

- Where do I experience my optimal operating state?

- Where is my life full of "get to's"? How can I have more?

- What will I do to grow my positivity?

When I am BIG . . .

Who am I when I'm BIG?

- *I set a goal and meet it; I start a project and finish it; I teach someone something new; I make someone laugh.*

- *I am a good boss, peer, employee, friend, and neighbor.*

- *I am a good son, brother, husband, and father.*

Those things are good and make me feel BIG. Yet I am just doing what I was meant to do. I am using my God-given talents and skills to be purposeful. But more than BIG, I feel thankful. Much of the above comes naturally. Not everyone is so fortunate.

Who am I when I'm BIG?

- *I am part of enabling others to shine, to help them to do great things and feel purposeful. Yet I stay in the background.*

- *I can marvel at the world around me. Not because I did anything specific, but because I am part of it. You would think that would make me feel small, but it doesn't. You can't fake marveling to yourself.*

- *I'm genuine, patient, and I truly listen, not just hear, and certainly do not do all the talking.*

These things are great and make me feel even BIGGER, but there is more.

Who am I when I'm BIG?

- I realize I've made a mistake, can admit it, and then learn from it.

- I can say I'm sorry, and mean it.

- I can forgive, unconditionally.

Those things are awesome. They are just for me, myself and I. They don't come from brains or brawn, they come from inside. They make me feel the BIGGEST.

Who am I when I'm BIG?

I put my head down on my pillow at night, close my eyes, and fall right to sleep, not because I'm tired or exhausted, but because I'm happy and comfortable with me, who I am and what I've done, especially those difficult things.

It doesn't happen every night, but when it does, not only do I feel BIG, but I dream BIG . . .

—PATRICK MORRISSEY
President and Principal Consultant,
Morrissey Consulting LLC

CHAPTER 5

Breaking through to **BIG**ness

"Who we are is who we are when we are not being who we are not."
—ANONYMOUS

Most of our clients, even those who are mega-successful, still hear negative voices within. They are lacking, at times, in gratitude, appreciation, and the ability to see what is right in their world. In working with senior leaders over the years, we clearly have seen that some of the most powerful and confident ones are dealing with such negativity. The distinction is that they are dealing with it. The goal is not to completely silence those negative voices, but rather to manage them.

As human beings, we all encounter limiting beliefs that surface in our minds. We become fearful, or doubtful, or anxious. We begin to play small. We operate out of scarcity. These limiting beliefs come in different sizes.

They can be very specific: You want to take a vacation, but that inner critic says, "If you take that time away, you'll come back and you won't have a job." Or they can be globally limiting: "I'm just not good enough. I cannot succeed. I don't deserve this relationship."

In order to really cultivate your BIGness, it is critical to turn down the volume on negative chatter.

Controlling who has the microphone

When you hear those voices, you can think of it as a management opportunity. You won't be getting rid of those voices forever, but you will be able to control who has the microphone in your mind. The key is awareness. If we don't know what is happening, then we risk being held hostage to the negativity and those limiting beliefs. Once you have awareness, you have the opportunity for greater freedom, and you are on the way to a breakthrough.

One client, who needed to network more within her company, was telling herself, "I'm not a natural people person." To meet her, you would never think that she was not a people person. As it turned out, she had believed that since she was in third grade when the most popular kid on the playground had been mean to her. This was holding her back. She was able to turn that message into,

"I like myself, and that is what matters."

Those voices can be quite dated, indeed. The bigger the limiting belief, it seems, the longer that voice has been there. When you notice what is happening, you are making progress in managing those messages. Let's say that you are starting your day in a positive mood and suddenly you feel as if a dark cloud has rolled over you, but you look out and it's a sunny day. We ask clients to get curious about what is happening at such moments. What brings on a foul mood? What's happening when they find themselves stuck?

Think of it as the way you're able to take your cranky computer back in time to the last point when it was operating well. "I was fine at breakfast," you can tell yourself, "so what happened to get me feeling like this?" Perhaps the boss came in and gave you a little feedback. Did you conclude, "He doesn't like me and my job is at risk, and I could end up unemployed, especially in times such as this. I'll lose my house. I'll lose my marriage." It's as if your mind has been hijacked by fear and doubt and all those limiting beliefs.

Wild places

Our emotions can take us to wild places. Maybe the boss just said, "This report could be better." What the boss meant was simply that the report could be better. But those words tapped into so much else in your mind.

Clients are sometimes determined to defend those limiting beliefs—but they cannot come up with real evidence to justify them, because they are made up. That in itself is what identifies a limiting belief. People become so vested in what they think is the truth that they are blinded to other possibilities. They may feel they are on the verge of being fired, and yet every performance review is stellar, and the boss has never approached to say, "You're just not cutting it here." They are reacting to phantoms of the mind.

> **Our emotions can take us to wild places.**

These thoughts limit people of all walks of life. If you can get past what is getting in your way, you can fulfill your potential. You need to cultivate your BIGness. How do you go about knowing yourself, and learning about those passions that lie untapped? How can you empower yourself to be your best at any moment of any day and consistently over time?

> **We're saying that we all have times when we become critical.**

Think of your limiting beliefs as being on a continuum. At one end is the inner critic, that internal negative voice. When we say that people hear voices, we're not saying they are schizophrenic or have multiple personalities. We're saying that we all have times when we become critical. We wag a finger at ourselves, the way some teacher or parent might have done. It's a powerful energy, but it limits us. We can become paralyzed by the resulting fear, doubt, and anxiety, and as a result we don't strive for the BIGness. That's one end of our continuum.

It's a powerful energy, but it limits us.

At the other end of the continuum is that positive voice of the Whisperer. It's a voice of the champion. It's the internal coach that those Olympians heeded. It's a voice of hope and possibility. This is where we hear what we call "powerful assumptions." They, too, are made up. They are products of the mind, but the gift is this: We can take that limiting belief and flip it. Instead of the energy of negativity, you have the energy of positivity.

The challenge for many is that it seems the inner critic has gone out and purchased a $250,000 sound system to produce so much noise in our heads that we are not able to hear the positive voice of the Whisperer, who is offering quiet wisdom. The inner critic is vested in the status quo and will produce fear and doubt in an attempt to paralyze you from going for your BIG. We have heard the language of our client's inner critics, and they scream stuff that you wouldn't say to your worst enemies. If we spoke to our children the way our inner critics speak to us internally, someone would notify Child Protective Services.

> **The negative and the positive both are merely frames of mind, but the latter is empowering. It's a real game changer.**

The critical voice says this: "I can never get that job. I'm not qualified." The Whisperer says, "I have the intelligence, drive, and passion to do that job effortlessly." Just imagine having a list of your powerful assumptions on your mirror in the morning as you're getting ready for the day, or as a screensaver on your computer. What's the probability your mood would shift? The negative and the positive both are merely frames of mind, but the latter is empowering. It's a real game changer.

From limiting to empowering

Our inner critic wants us to forget about the positives. Try this: No matter where you are, if a limiting belief comes along, write it down—on a napkin at a restaurant, if need be—and get it onto paper and out of your head. That way, you can challenge it later. Otherwise, it will keep bouncing around in your brain. The trick is to take note of it and realize, "Just look at what I am saying to myself." In doing so, you take away at least some of the power of that negative voice.

We ask clients to think of these two personalities, the Critic and the Whisperer, as if they were characters on a movie set. What do they look like? Are they male? Are they female? What kind of energy do they give off? We ask them to name them. The more clearly we can define them, the more we can understand which one has the microphone. "Oh, that's just my Critic," we can say, or "that's my Whisperer." People get highly creative as they give names to those personas. Doing so can lighten the mood and make them feel easier to manage. It's an easy, light, and playful way to simply notice and take control. The Critic wants you to think this is a difficult chore. If you keep things whimsical, you help to take away its power. The smarter we are, the more sophisticated the Critic becomes in its arsenal as it tries to sabotage our lives.

Remember that we don't ever get rid of that negative voice. The goal is to manage it. We can learn to recognize our limiting beliefs and flip them into powerful assumptions. When the Critic lobs a limiting belief at you, you can be thrown out of that optimal operating state. The real challenge is how quickly you can reset yourself, return to BIG, so that you are doing your best work, your best communicating, and your best relating.

> **Remember that we don't ever get rid of that negative voice. The goal is to manage it. We can learn to recognize our limiting beliefs and flip them into powerful assumptions.**

It is an interesting dance to watch as people attempt to create powerful assumptions. We notice that they find it easy to create robust limiting beliefs, but when we ask them to create a powerful assumption, very few nail it the first time out.

On the way to a powerful assumption is a positive assumption. If the limiting belief is, "I'll never be able to find the love of my life," a positive assumption might be, "I will find the love of my life." But there's no energy in that. There's no power in that. It becomes a powerful assumption when you say, "With the passion and the humor and the ability to love the way I know I can, I can create a magical and loving relationship."

It puts you in a different place when you are dating.

"What if this person doesn't like me?" becomes, "I'm going to humor this person and I'm going to love the way I know how." You can imagine how the latter mindset moves things along quite differently.

Reality check

Some people insist that the critical voice is simply reality. That's how much they have bought in to the message being true. Even when clients hold fast to that perception, we at least can help them see the opportunity to focus on the issue and get it behind them.

Can we control everything? Absolutely not. Life can happen at any moment, good, bad, or ugly. And, yes, in this day and age, people can lose their jobs seemingly at the snap of a finger. You can call that reality, but do we want to go through life in a cautious, negative state, always looking out for something bad that's going to happen and perhaps even bring it on? Or do we rewire ourselves so that we see it all as part of the ride? What we can control is how we respond, and we can choose the

> *You can choose to navigate as you ride the rapids down the river, and it will be a thrill, or you can just let yourself be dashed against the rocks.*

mindset and the mood that we choose to wake up with every morning.

In other words, you can choose to navigate as you ride the rapids down the river, and it will be a thrill, or you can just let yourself be dashed against the rocks. Either way would be a reality. But one choice is empowering, and the other could batter your body and drown you.

Whenever a client who has lost a job laments his fate, we can offer a guarantee: If you hold out the possibility that good things will come, your life is going to get exponentially better. In the moment, it's painful. It's like grieving a loss. But you can also think of it as a beginning. Instead of operating out of fear, this can be a time when you boldly step out to try a new strategy, get a new skill.

This can be a time of awakening. In a few years, you could look back and be grateful because it forced your hand. In the meantime, you can try to envision what good could come out of this hardship and start reaching for it. This is the time when you get to pause and take a breath. Free of the workaholic stress, you can reconnect with family—your children, your spouse, your aging parents. You don't have to miss out on those joys. It can give you the perspective to decide whether you want to go back to doing exactly what you did before in your career—or perhaps focus on whatever aspect of it you enjoyed. This can be your breakthrough to BIGness.

Take time to be mindful

Give yourself that break. If your Critic is chattering loudly, give yourself a daily 120 seconds of silence in which you are unplugged and can be mindful of what the Whisperer is saying to you. "Unplugged" doesn't mean you are listening to music, or working out. It means your eyes are closed, and you are focused on breathing. Once you give yourself those two minutes a day, you may find yourself wanting ten minutes, and more. Eastern cultures have seen the value of meditation for thousands of years. Certainly we can practice a little daily mindfulness.

We're not suggesting you turn into a yogi. We're suggesting you clear your head. If you are running fast with all that noise in your head, you can't hear those glimmers of possibilities, those innovative and creative ideas that are informing what might be next for you. We need more time with just ourselves in this very loud world.

Researchers have actually found that doing so seems to enhance the regions of the brain that control creativity and innovation. That's a poignant and fascinating finding. It illustrates what we are doing to ourselves in this fast-paced, to-do-list world, where technology beeps at us all day long. We are under endless stress, and the Critic thrives on that. The Whisperer helps us to stay BIG through it all, and mindfulness allows us to hear that soothing voice.

You can download an app called the Therapeutic Zone or the Breathing Zone—it's called both. It takes you through five minutes of gazing at a colorful circle that contracts and expands, helping you to pace your breathing. It's a great tool for your daily unplugging, or meditating, or whatever you want to call that time when you free your mind from distractions so that you can tap into things.

Bill Gross, founder of PIMCO, is one of the largest active global fixed income investment managers in the world. In a CNN interview, he stated,

> *The most important part of my day isn't on the trading floor. Every day at 8:30 A.M., I get up from my desk and walk to a health club across the street. I do yoga and work out for probably an hour and a half, between 8:30 and 10. There's only been two or three times in the past 30 years when someone has come across the street and told me I should get back to the office. One of them was the 1987 market crash.*

There's an understanding here that that's my haven. Some of my best ideas literally come from standing on my head doing yoga. I'm away from the office, away from the noise, away from the Bloomberg screens—not to mention that standing on your head increases the blood flow to your brain.

After about 45 minutes of riding the exercise bike and maybe ten or 15 minutes of yoga, all of a sudden some significant light bulbs seem to turn on. I look at that hour and a half as the most valuable time of the day.

In doing so, in the middle of prime trading time, he turns off the external noise. His track record of success attests to the value of such discipline.

Each of us must find our own way that works. Some people are wired for meditation. Extroverts, however, who thrive on engaging with others, can find it more challenging to be alone. They actually may feel that it depletes their energy. If that describes you, you can try guided meditation, and there are numerous apps available that help you develop the discipline for a half hour of silence. The point is to give your mind the rest it needs to flourish.

BIG INSIGHTS:

- When does my inner critic grab the microphone?

- What is it saying?

- What is a more powerful perspective?

- Where and when can I unplug on a daily basis for 120 seconds or more?

When I am BIG. . .

When I am BIG . . .
My work seems like play and I can get lost in it for hours.
The bigger the problem, the more creative I become when solving it.
I lead with integrity, and I'm a good team member.
I'm confident.

When I am BIG . . .
I'm always looking for opportunities to learn something new.
I listen twice as much as I talk.
I'm a good mentor and give what I believe to be the best advice, even
*   if it goes against my own best interests.*

When I am BIG . . .
I'm strong in the face of adversity.
I use wisdom to make decisions based on what would be best in the
*   long run.*
I maintain my sense of humor even in the darkest times.
I keep my word, regardless of consequences, and I keep my
*   commitments simple: My "yes" means yes and my "no" means no.*

When I am BIG . . .

I keep myself healthy as much as it depends on me.
I eat right, exercise regularly, and get plenty of rest.
I understand that my body is my vehicle, and if it doesn't work well,
*   then it will hinder me in fulfilling my purpose in life.*

When I am BIG . . .

I'm in tune with my God, I know my purpose in life and I keep it as
*   my primary objective.*
I'm compassionate.
I'm generous with my time and money, and I use my skills and
*   abilities to help others who can't help themselves.*

When I am BIG . . .

I can look into the eyes of an innocent child and see my own
*   reflection.*
I'm in line with my life plan, and I maintain a balanced life.

—BOB HULL
Direct Marketing Consultant
Noble Direct Marketing

CHAPTER 6

Allan's story: The best gig on the planet

You have heard some of my story in the introduction chapter, "The secret of the champions." The rest of my story follows.

Once when I was a kid in Kalamazoo, Michigan, I was down by the creek with my brother and several friends. We began to talk, as kids do, about what we were going to do when we grew up.

"I'm going to go into sales," Bill said with confidence.

"I'm going to be a teacher," said Ann Marie.

"I'll be a nurse," offered Beth.

"I want to be a mechanic," said Scott.

My turn. Silence. I figured I just hadn't gotten the chip that programs what one will do in life. I just turned to them and asked how they could possibly know so soon.

My brother and I ended up leaving Kalamazoo, but I'm grateful for that Midwest upbringing and the values that came with it. You could leave your door unlocked, and everyone in the neighborhood knew you. It was a simple, happy time.

I went to a private liberal arts college, one of the top six in the country. It was a unique college, because you lived abroad for a year and you worked in what you thought your career was going to be. Back then, I thought I was going to be a banker, and thank goodness the experience nailed that coffin shut for me.

I graduated with a psychology degree, and my thesis in my senior year was on humanistic management. So there were clues that I would be somehow involved in dealing with people and human potential.

But the calling didn't begin to truly come together until I was probably 31. I climbed the ladder in the hospitality industry and then moved to a fourteen-person engineering environment in Silicon Valley. In retrospect, it should have been a clue that this was not a Bold Move, as it took me three months of negotiations before accepting the offer. I had moved from work in a well-oiled machine to a bootstrap start-up. The product didn't get off the ground as we had hoped during the year I was there—and it felt as if a part of me was dying. I was so committed to success and attempting to look good to the external world that I couldn't accept failure.

One year to the day after I was hired, the president came to me and asked, "How is this working?" My response was, "It's not," and he agreed. It was awkward, as we were friends, but it was apparent to both of us that this was not a match.

I remember feeling a lot of shame. I left the office and drove over the San Francisco Bay Bridge. The skies were the bluest of blue. The cityscape looked like Oz as the sun rose over the bay and the water shimmered. It was 9:20 in the morning. I felt a voice inside me saying, "You know, this is an important day for you, and you are going to do just fine." It was a whisper of hope and possibility.

Growing up, I had been the best little boy, living to make everyone happy. Upon realizing that my job wasn't working out, I felt that old twinge of shame and disappointment. But now, I also felt a lightness of relief. I could now enter the major path of my life.

It had been a long way from Kalamazoo to the Bay Bridge.

I began to ask myself, for the very first time, where I was heading. My thoughts went like this: "Allan, what do *you* want to do? You have listened intently to what the external world thinks you ought to have done, but what's important to *you?*" All signs pointed to a career in human development, helping people to reach their potential.

> **"Allan, what do you want to do? You have listened intently to what the external world thinks you ought to have done, but what's important to you?"**

I had saved money, and I began researching schools for a graduate degree. One school seemed perfect, as if it were designed for me, and I embarked on a three-year graduate program in counseling psychology and holistic health in the Bay Area. Later, I began my work at Drake Beam Morin as a career consultant as I finished my degree.

The concept of "Who are you when you are BIG?" came to me when I was a career consultant at DBM. Companies would hire us to work with executives whom they were laying off for one reason or another. Many had no idea, for the first time, where their career was headed next. All of a sudden, that business card was gone. It was humbling to watch defeated middle-aged executives enter into my office. In our initial sessions, I would ask them to consider the office to be a white room—sort of like the *Star Trek* "holodeck," where anything was possible.

That was when I began coaching, even though I was there as a career consultant. I saw an opportunity. I tried to make people feel more relaxed. Most of the offices had standard fluorescent ceiling lights, but I had a soft lamp and an ornamental fountain and a cozier, soothing setting. I could lean in to people when they were feeling vulnerable and ask some big questions. I went beyond the career context. I asked what they thought about their lives. I got them thinking about just who they were and who they could be—their greatest accomplishments, their early dreams. *Who were they when they were BIG?*

It got to the point where new clients would ask to work with me even before visiting the office. Something magical was happening. People felt valued for who they really were, and they opened themselves to possibilities they had never considered. They imagined what life could be like. It was an amazing journey as those people transitioned. To me, it was just the magic of the coaching. We were uncovering people's potential and gifts and encouraging them to go for what they wanted.

Later, my wife brought leadership coaching into her company—she was a leader in the hospitality industry for the Bay Area—and one day she said to me, "You know, I've met the founders of a coaching school, and the three of you are so much alike—you've just got to meet these people!"

"These people" were Karen and Henry Kimsey-House, the co-founders of CTI. Back then, they were personally running the programs.

I'm told that working as a career consultant is a great way to launch into a successful coaching business, and I had been dealing with top performers. My first coaching client was a partner at PricewaterhouseCoopers, who wanted to expand her interests. From there, the word spread. That was the beginning of a career that has grown by 100 percent word of mouth.

I completed my coach training with CTI in 1998, which is when I began my coaching business, and I have never looked back. I love what I do, and I'm excited that I "get to" go to work. I haven't always felt that way. I'm humbled by this turn of events, given the fact that for so long I had no clue whether I would ever find a meaningful and purposeful career.

What I loved about career consulting was that clients were motivated to move forward, particularly since they needed to make a living and pay the bills. It was a pleasure to help them find an alignment between a lucrative career and one that played to their strengths and passions. I found my niche when I spring-boarded from there into the coaching model that has served me.

At long last, I figured out what I wanted to be when I grew up. I have found what for me is the best gig on the planet. I wake up and feel privileged for what I get to do. In more ways than one, it is my livelihood.

I only wish that when I was a kid, someone had showed me how to discover and express the BIG in myself. I believe adults have a responsibility to help steward young people to learn what is uniquely meaningful to them. Unless we encourage them to look deeply into their hearts, many will let the world tell them who and what they should be—right down to the kind of car they should drive and the clothes they should wear.

Drop the heavy weights— BIG is light and easy

For whatever reason, I couldn't read even when I was eight years old. The psychologists recommended that I be removed from my family and put into a military academy next to a Nazarene College with an excellent reading program for children. The academy was run by nuns—interesting because I was not raised Catholic. In those days, many parents gave their authority away to the professionals. My mother didn't like it, but she figured that's what you do. I was there for three years, and I did learn to read, but it took me decades to recover from the feelings of rejection and abandonment. Why had I been shipped away?

> **Every one of us is shaped by the past, but it's the future that matters now.**

We all have our stories. We all have faced difficulty and unpleasantness. Some people define themselves by those stories. They look in the mirror, and they see only shortcomings and judgments and criticisms that block any reflection of the amazing gifts they could offer the world. I'm here to say that we no longer need to let life get us down or hold us back. There are other stories of victory and joy, and those are the ones that will propel us forward to greater things.

Every one of us is shaped by the past, but it's the future that matters now. We need to find out what is inside of us and release that potential. We can't live on autopilot. It's time to live intentionally. The world awaits our courage.

We look around us at a world in crisis and we wonder. We wonder daily as the news reports come in. And in our interconnected world, we have unprecedented collective power to do something about it—if only we would take the initiative. People increasingly look at

> **The world awaits our courage.**

their lives and say, "There's something way bigger that I'm supposed to be doing, and it ain't this." Helping people step into being BIG is, I believe, what this book is all about.

BIG INSIGHTS:

- What would my "best gig" look like?

- How can I be BIGger in my current work?

- What clues are within me related to my next Bold Move?

When I am BIG . . .

I awake . . .
in a mood of positivity and possibility for the day
curious for the day
humbled to do what I chose to do to make a difference
grateful for those in my life
feeling the abundance of purposeful work

I believe . . .
that I can do whatever my mind tells me
when I focus on the 'what' of my dreams, the 'how' will inform
   itself
I can make a profound difference
something greater than me is showing me the right path
I am on this planet to heal, ignite, and activate human potential
anything is possible

I tap into . . .
wonderful humor that makes me laugh at myself
the ability to feel and emote
something bigger than me that serves
an energy that heals
the courage to trust

My relationship as a . . .
father allows me to feel profound unconditional love
husband allows me to love and be loved through vulnerability
son allows me acceptance that physical life is not eternal
brother allows me to lean into compassion
friend has me showing up authentically with humor, care, and
   compassion
coach allows me to hold the BIGness in my clients

When I am BIG, I can let go of the need to worry, judge, fix,
second-guess, feel less than, question, compare, be fearful.
When I am BIG, I feel love.

—ALLAN MILHAM

CHAPTER 7

From surviving to thriving **BIG**

The client came in with a simple request: He wanted some help with how to handle himself on a job interview. He had a list of potential questions that he might be asked, and for each he had written out long responses, which he had essentially memorized. He was woefully over prepared. He was making poor eye contact, and he seemed very nervous.

The one thing that he said he felt most prepared to talk about during an interview was his greatest accomplishment. He related his story about starting an IT department from scratch. It was a spinoff from the company he had worked for, and he was appointed CIO. He hired a team of 57 people, as well as some outside contractors to supplement the team during the building phase. It was essential that the project be done on time and on budget, and they had managed to do so.

He spoke about this in a monotone, though he had

improved his eye contact. There was no energy behind his words, no emphasis. We decided that he would tell the story again—but this time, making it sound as if it truly were the great accomplishment that he said it was. Could he present this as if he were proud of what he had done?

In his second telling, he droned out his memorized words in much the same monotone. It was if he had taken an organizational chart out of a textbook and plugged names into the boxes. So what was so special about his tale? We cut short his retelling the story and just chatted about this accomplishment.

It turned out that he felt the subcontractors hadn't been treating his team with respect, and when they didn't change their ways after he warned them, he ended their contract. His team then found a new energy and rose to the occasion, getting the project done not only on time but also under budget, since there were no subcontractors to pay. As he related several other stories, a theme emerged: He created teams that delivered, and in the IT world projects often tend to come in over budget and late.

What was remarkable was the way his eyes sparkled when he was talking about his team. His face beamed with pride. It was clear that they had inspired him and that he had inspired them. His story revealed, without his saying so, that he was a great leader. He could hire a great team. He would do the right things. He understood what "on time, on budget" meant. He knew how to handle outside subcontractors. A simple story showed so much about him—we had tapped into his qualities, his gifts.

Proudest moments

When we ask people about their proudest moments, we suggest that they think of a time when they truly felt that they were in their element. If they try to relate something from the head and not the heart, they will tend to focus on what the interviewer wants to hear, or what they think would sound good. Their story may be told from a place of big ego. Far better if the accomplishment truly evoked pride, deep in the soul—from the place of heart ego. Far better if the accomplishment felt easy, effortless, fun.

In other words, we want people to tap into a time when they were truly thriving, not a time when they were just surviving or still striving. When you are surviving, you are on autopilot, not really thinking anything through. You presume you're doing the right stuff. You're climbing the ladder. You're doing all the things you thought you were supposed to be doing, and it's drive, drive, drive.

By contrast, when you are thriving, you are more attuned to your life purpose, and the dividend is inner peace. You are living who you are.

> **When you are thriving, you are more attuned to your life purpose, and the dividend is inner peace. You are living who you are.**

We've had clients speak of their "greatest accomplishments"—big projects, high profile, high stakes, and awards. But when we ask them about the day-to-day nature of the experience, sometimes we find it was miserable.

"I've always known how it feels to be surviving," another client said, "and now, I know what it means to be thriving." She had a way of looking up at the sky when she was deep in thought, as if for direction. Fittingly, the name she gave to her Whisperer was "Sky Pilot." She had been able to shift her mindset from one of just getting by, of just surviving, so that she could have a purposeful and fulfilling life.

In the boot camps, participants are asked to come up with several accounts of a time when they were thriving, focusing on these questions: What was the situation? What was the action? What was the result? And, most importantly, why was it so meaningful?

When you're coming from your proudest moment, there's meaning in it. When you're coming from your greatest sounding accomplishment, there may or may not have been meaning in it. Yes, you accomplished it, but it might have been miserable.

People often have trouble thinking back to these times. It's hard for them. An approach that helps them is to come up with one good story, and then think about the feeling that arose in them. What other times have they ever felt that way? By focusing on the feeling, they often more readily can tap into times when they were thriving. They are remembering with the heart instead of the head.

> **By understanding who you are and what is unique about you when you are thriving, you can be confident about what you want others to see in you.**

After the boot campers come up with their stories, their next step is to ask what their stories have in common. Each participant is asked to consider what three headlines could be written about them, what five words would sum them up, or what kind of metaphor arises. What distinguishes them when they are thriving? How are they unique?

That is the essence of personal brand management. In drawing conclusions about their stories, the boot camp participants are, in effect, identifying their brand.

In short, we need to be sure that how other people view us is the way that we intend for them to view us. By understanding who you are and what is unique about you when you are thriving, you can be confident about what you want others to see in you. You should want them to see who you truly are, not just what you have done.

Being BIG with your brand

Another executive, a chief financial officer, was developing his brand and had pulled together his accounts of times when he felt that he was thriving. He had been an Eagle Scout, and what we realized in examining his stories of his proudest moments was this: He was the Eagle Scout of CFOs.

He wasn't just the executive who saved a big company millions of dollars, which sounds so remarkably similar to so many others. Instead, we realized that what he projected as a brand was this: He was *loyal* and *trustworthy* in getting the books right. He was *thrifty* and the books were "*clean*." He was big on internal controls and the reliability of the financial information and getting things done on time and on budget and not missing deadlines. He was the good and responsible CFO. And he was an adventurous sort too—*brave* like a good Scout: He wanted to work on transactions that would change the face of the company, or double business through acquisitions. He wanted to do work that would have meaning to the company on a grander scale. He also worked with his team in a way that was *helpful, cheerful, kind,* and *courteous* to his team. All traits of an Eagle Scout.

His life-long identity as an Eagle Scout translated into the type of leader he was. That was indeed his brand. By looking at his proudest moments, he had identified the essence of who he was. By looking at a time when he was thriving, he had mapped his way to a future of far more than surviving.

Tigger is BIGger—managing your brand

Sometimes the people who have trouble maintaining a brand are highly successful. They're overachievers or they're overcommitted or they have demanding jobs. They have great intentions, but pressure and frustrations get in the way, and they can feel overwhelmed—and the stress shows. Sure, they may be grounded most of the time, but those stress behaviors are what people often remember. We judge ourselves by our intentions, others judge us by our actions, and brand management is keeping our intentions and actions in sync.

If you are like many people, you may have one personality perhaps 80 percent of the time when things are going well for you, and you may have quite another for 20 percent of the time when you feel stressed or overwhelmed or frustrated. Unfortunately, people who observe you in that down time will remember that and may tend to identify you by that.

> **Tigger is a Whisperer, and Eeyore is a Critic.**

That's why it's so important to identify your brand and to understand what you are projecting. For example, to borrow characters from A. A. Milne's Winnie the Pooh tales, you would likely want to be known as a Tigger, not as an Eeyore. Tigger is an optimistic tiger, full of energy and enthusiasm. Eeyore is a sad sack donkey, weary and woeful. Tigger emits positive energy. He projects hope and possibility, and he dreams. Eeyore emits negative energy. He projects difficulty and defeat, and he criticizes. Tigger is a Whisperer, and Eeyore is a Critic.

Do you present yourself to the world as an upbeat problem solver? Are you someone who always comes up with the ideas, or are you someone who squelches them? Perhaps you walk around saying, "I'm so tired," or, "I'm so busy," to the point where people think, "Right, we're all tired and busy, but he thinks he's more important, I guess."

Ask yourself whether you want your brand to be one who looks for what's right or who looks for what's wrong? One who handles stress well, or who freaks out? As you develop your personal brand, you have a choice.

When people are introduced to the concept of personal brand management, they begin to wonder. They start asking themselves questions such as, "Who am I being?" and, "How am I coming across in this world?" It might be at work, it might be when they get home from work, it might be with the kids, it might be with their spouse— but in any number of ways, they start to see themselves through others' eyes. They had viewed themselves as hardworking, loyal, and dedicated. Others might have seen a person frustrated, stressed out, overwhelmed.

One client, a busy executive, said she cried for a week after realizing how colleagues perceived her. She took her role quite seriously, feeling a weight of responsibility and always looking for the ultimate good of the company. She was something of a perfectionist, as well, and she spoke up when she thought the company was going down the wrong path. She felt compelled to tell senior management and all the people around her. What she had come to realize during coaching was that she had developed a brand as "mean girl." But that was an important step for her. She became aware. That wasn't who she wanted to be for people, so she learned to bite her tongue at times and get her point across in different ways. She learned to first acknowledge what's right and explain why she was bringing up a point. The change in her was magical—and it started with awareness.

Finding your core values

You can think of being BIG as an inside-out proposition: It is tied to the core of who you are, and it is an expression of the values, beliefs, and principles most special to you. To thrive, you need to define those. We ask new clients to think about that, and to envision their legacy. It's not always easy. Many people have never thought specifically about their core values and beliefs, but it is important to be curious about them, because they inform your legacy and purpose.

> *You can think of being BIG as an inside-out proposition: It is tied to the core of who you are, and it is an expression of the values, beliefs, and principles most special to you.*

Some get ideas for their list by searching online for the word "values." That's one place to start, but in narrowing down the many possibilities you will find on the Internet, be sure to choose the words that describe the unique you. Don't simply pick out attributes that you think you *should* pick. This is no time to be on autopilot.

Once you have gathered some ideas on your values, consider asking others who are close to you—your spouse or colleagues you trust—to share how they see you. They may be able to help you identify things that you may not see in yourself.

However you define or collect your top values, we believe they are central and essential to your definition of who you are when you are BIG. We both work with people who place high importance on their careers, and they are generally compensated well. Frequently, however, the executives we coach have been on autopilot before working with us. It's true that core values generally do not change over time, but their meaning certainly can be refined.

Sue was a client who told the following story about a key revelation related to her values:

> *I grew up in a home of a single mother with no*
> *college degree raising four kids, and one of the*

things that was instilled in me as my top value was independence—that a woman should always be able to be independent. Even my father instilled the value in me as he saw my mother struggle, and as he saw me as a very capable person who could do anything.

For many years, this value served me very well. I succeeded in college and graduated summa cum laude. I went on to be recruited into a premier position in a major corporation. I succeeded in making it to the executive level and ultimately to the C-suite. I married a wonderful man who was also at the top of his game in corporate America. We were living an affluent life. Yet my husband and I both readily admitted that we were married first to our jobs, and only secondly to each other!

What I came to realize later as a result of coaching was that "independence" all those years as my number-one value had meant financial independence. While my husband appreciated my independence, he also viewed me as very controlling. I didn't need him to do anything for me. Ironically, he shows his love through service and through providing for me.

I was oblivious that this was something very core to most men. I couldn't let his love in with my fierce independence. I never meant to be emotionally independent. Love and the capacity to be loved was a far greater true value of mine than how I was defining independence.

Anytime we see leaders who are feeling burned out, it immediately indicates to us that something in their life is at odds with their values. Perhaps they have been too engrossed in a project at work, and their family life is suffering. Perhaps they are working diligently on work that is not meaningful to them. Perhaps they have stopped learning and growing professionally and personally. Perhaps they perceive that their work is no longer providing them with challenging opportunities. Perhaps they are neglecting their health and their bodies, and their doctors are screaming back at them.

Wheel of Life and priorities

The Wheel of Life is a tool we commonly use with our clients to measure their level of satisfaction in key areas of their life. On a scale of 1 to 10 they rate their level of satisfaction with each of the following: career, money, health, family and friends, significant other/romance, personal growth, fun and recreation, and physical environment. This tool can often give us some clues about the holistic view of the client and things they may want to address as part of our coaching. When their "wheel" is jagged—meaning they have diverse ratings on their levels of satisfaction—they generally are not in balance with their values.

> **Anytime we see leaders who are feeling burned out, it immediately indicates to us that something in their life is at odds with their values.**

We can take this a step further and ask our clients to rate the level of importance of each of the categories. Almost invariably, health and family relationships appear at the top of the priority list. If we then ask them to rate the relative amount of time or effort they devote to each category, career and money almost invariably end up at the top of the list. Unfortunately, it is not uncommon for health to fall at the bottom and family relationships to fall in the middle or at the bottom.

Legacy and purpose

Before we learned to live intentionally, if someone had asked us about our legacy or purpose, the question would have seemed esoteric—"You want me to think about *what*?" That's a common response from coaching clients in our early conversations. But if we are to live intentionally and with meaning, we must decide how we want to live and how we want to be known—not just on any given day, but for a lifetime. The question of why you are here is central to understanding who you are when you are BIG.

What we know to be true is that core values, once defined and planted, seem to stay with us over time. However, our legacy and purpose shift with these core values as we mature and gain greater consciousness and clarity.

Defining your purpose and core values also allows for your Whisperer to keep a stronger grip on the microphone, and in many ways will contribute to the richness of your experience as you get in touch with who you are when you are BIG. There is far more about this topic than we can adequately present on these pages.

BIG INSIGHTS:

- **Where have I thrived in the past—what was meaningful about it?**

- **What is my intended personal brand? What is my actual brand?**

- **What are my core values and beliefs and where is my life out of synch with those?**

- **How do I want to be known—not just for today, but for a lifetime?**

- **What's right that I can amplify in my life?**

When I am Big . . .

When I'm BIG, I live at the crossroads of opportunity and giftedness; it's a place where my education and experience, my talents and passion are deployed in such a way that my daily work is transformed into my life's calling;

When I'm BIG, I help an organization discover and clarify its mission, define and design its strategy, and align investment so that financial performance is a natural consequence of mission fulfillment and not the primary objective.

When I'm BIG, I'm with other people who are BIG too, and together we collaborate and work in such a way that accomplishes both corporate and individual goals; I develop not just products and processes, but people as well;

When I'm BIG, my day begins before the alarm goes off, excited about the prospect of a brand new day and hoping that being BIG gives way to being huge; not just as a professional but as a husband, father, and friend, as well;

When I'm BIG, every fiber of my being is fully being the person that God has designed me to be.

*That's what I look like when **I am BIG**.*

—FRANK BORST
Chief Operating Officer
Vintage Senior Living

CHAPTER 8

Leading
from **BIG**

Leadership is about far more than how you conduct yourself with others in your career and on the job. You are a leader in your family, in your community—in your life.

As executive coaches, we deal primarily with top-performing business leaders, but let us be clear that the concept of BIG applies as well to the mom or dad whose job is not at the office from 9 to 5, but rather who has the around-the-clock responsibilities of tending to a family. Each can have very different views of the world, with different definitions of the demands of leadership, and yet both in earnest can be yearning to find out who they truly are when they are BIG.

Authentic leadership emanates from the inside. It is values based, arising from your core beliefs. At some point, those beliefs and those values plug into a vision and a desire to get activated.

We understand that when we are dealing with leaders, we are not dealing with part of a person. We are working with the whole leader—and playing an important role in that leadership is what's going on in his or her personal life, with family or marriage and the multitude of issues that people face day by day. Those have a profound effect on work and career.

> **Authentic leadership emanates from the inside. It is values based, arising from your core beliefs.**

A coach can't just shrug off the personal side of someone and deal only with who shows up at work. To understand the behaviors at work, we have to address all that the person is going through. Your values are deeper than your work life and your work behaviors, and they inform what is happening.

As we discussed in the last chapter, when someone is stuck or struggling in his or her career, there is often a misalignment with what is at his or her core. To get unstuck, you need to come into a deeper understanding of that. Then you can experience the empowerment that will allow you to move forward to even more effective leadership.

We've both worked with numerous high-performing

executives whose primary identity had become their work. They may have come to us because they were feeling overwhelmed, because they were dissatisfied or feeling stuck, or because their stress behaviors were getting in their way. It's not uncommon for us to discover they may have been engrossed in work as a way to avoid something in their personal lives, such as a troubled marriage or family issues, which was creating issues that carried over to their work place. In finding out who you are when we are BIG, you need to face life's challenges, not avoid them.

Leading yourself first

Before you ever can expect others to fall in line with you, you must establish a vision for yourself. You need to know where you are going and feel that drive within you. In short, good leaders must be self-aware and able to manage, above all, themselves.

Leading from BIG is a courageous move, and a bold one. It takes courage just to be in the conversation. You need to know your core beliefs and values so that you can seed and nurture a vision and make it happen. We are given the opportunity to assume leadership to pursue what we want. It's a gift.

The root of the word "courage" is the Latin *cor*, meaning

heart—and that's quite fitting when we talk about the kind of leadership that requires not just leading from the head but from the whole of who we are. It can take courage to lead from the heart—it certainly is not the norm. To lead from the heart is to lead from love and compassion, and that's what makes the difference between average leaders and great leaders. We like to think of it as "heart-rage."

> **The root of the word "courage" is the Latin cor, meaning heart—and that's quite fitting when we talk about the kind of leadership that requires not just leading from the head but from the whole of who we are.**

A recent *Forbes* article examined people's workplace fears, and one of them is that they feel they cannot be themselves in the workplace. But those who manage to lead from BIG will take a stand to be authentic and transparent, and they will lead from there. They have the heart to be great. If BIG were an acronym, we like to think it would stand for Believing in Greatness.

The best leaders embrace a belief, and they come with courage. They know their values. They have the wherewithal to be able to seed and implement visions so that people really want to be around them. They release a positive energy that spreads to others. They establish a company culture in which that energy thrives— and where employees certainly feel comfortable to be themselves.

One highly successful client had a daughter who graduated from college, went to Italy for a couple of years, and then came home to sit on her dad's couch, unemployed, or at least that was what his inner critic was telling him. He was worried that she wasn't achieving her potential. He felt compelled to play the parent role. It was a "do this, try that" directive role, albeit soft, and he knew that he had his daughter's best interest in mind. But he was motivated by fear that she was stuck and directionless. He's a tremendous father. His actions in those moments weren't coming from his values. It was clear he believed in her, and when asked what was right about her, he saw a strong, independent woman who had the courage to live a few years in a foreign country. She was just unclear where she wanted to go with her career. A parent who views a child from a perspective of faith instead of fear takes a much different approach. It's an approach that is more likely to motivate change. She is now enrolled in a pre-med program and on her way to becoming a doctor.

Nobody wants to be directed or cajoled into action.

People want to feel that they make things happen of their own volition, and powerful leaders have the gift of encouragement. They are servant leaders who are clear about what they stand for—they have led themselves first—and now they are interested in fostering the greatness in those whom they lead. They are not constantly trying to fix what they see as broken or helping those whom they think are helpless.

Managing those emotions

To be emotionally intelligent, we must first be self-aware. We need to be aware of those inner voices that can either motivate or derail us. Then we must self-manage. Once we are aware, we need to know how to choose to respond deliberately and intentionally. For example, as soon as the client was able to identify fear as the emotion behind his feelings toward his daughter, he was easily able to choose a different tack with her, one that came from his heart and not his head, and his daughter felt more supported.

Once people understand their inner critic and recognize those negative voices, they are able to be more mindful of what is getting in the way. Through self-management, they are better able to tap into positive emotions again. They are back in touch with their values and their vision.

When we say that leading from BIG is a courageous act, that doesn't mean you will be without doubts and fear. What you can do is manage those emotions, recognizing their source and put them in perspective so that the positive energy carries you forward.

Who is in your circle?

An easy way to self-management is to examine who is in your world. Who is in your circle? With whom do you hang? You will recall our earlier discussion of Barely, Brash, and Bold Move makers. Think of the people who you have around you. Make an honest assessment. If they are in the "barely" and "brash" camps, then they will have an orientation of fear and doubt. That is likely to have an impact on how you lead your own life and the quality of your life. Cultivating your friends and associates is an important choice. If you have naysayers around you telling you, "No, you can't," then they can hamper that spirit of boldness, the voice of the champion who says, "Yes, you can."

Most every parent has felt concern about a child's choice of friends. We want our children to stay clear of trouble and get involved in activities that will serve them for life. But parents should also be looking at their own circle. It's not that incorrigible naysayers are a bad element who will lead us astray, necessarily, but they could well be holding us back from realizing our full potential. If you aspire to strong leadership, you must pay attention to who influences you. If you wish to develop a powerful personal brand for your leadership, you must understand that those who surround you will become a part of it. Choose them well. Think BIG.

> *It's not that incorrigible naysayers are a bad element who will lead us astray, necessarily, but they could well be holding us back from realizing our full potential.*

Authentic leaders allow themselves to be transparent and vulnerable. They know what they stand for, and their actions are in line with their values. In doing so, they attract others to them who can share those values.

When you have vision, you are energizing people. As you consider your brand, think about who energizes you and whom you energize. Do you engage others, or are you more of a drain on them? If you truly are operating from BIG, you can be sure that you will be energizing people. There's no way you cannot. The right people will be drawn to you. Good leaders understand that.

It can be BIG to be vulnerable

Vulnerability can be scary at first. We get that. However, a word that was invisible in the workplace a generation ago is a bit of a secret weapon in the new paradigm of leadership. When we have the ability to demonstrate vulnerability, it shows the humanness in our leadership—a quality that actually inspires.

In today's world, people want to see leaders who don't think they have the answer to everything. They don't want leaders who come across as know-it-alls. Colleagues in a team meeting appreciate when a leader admits that he or she doesn't have the answer, but empowers the team to find one or take accountability to get an answer. It is interesting that when leaders are able to show their vulnerability, they will have followers with far more commitment and trust.

> **So many of us have been trained not to display vulnerability, and yet it is considered to be a top trait in leaders today, demonstrating emotional range and confidence.**

Fascinating research on vulnerability has come to the forefront, particularly Brené Brown's work on vulnerability and shame. As she says, "Vulnerability is the first thing I look for when I meet you, and the last thing I want to share with you." In her book *Daring Greatly*, Brown makes the case that vulnerability is not a weakness. She says we must dare to let ourselves be seen for who we truly are. That, she says, "is daring greatly."

So many of us have been trained not to display vulnerability, and yet it is considered to be a top trait in leaders today, demonstrating emotional range and confidence. Each of us keeps a veil over things we feel others don't need to know. When we are BIG, we become more willing to share that part of us. Behind the veil, your BIG awaits.

Your inner critic, meanwhile, will push back, suggesting to you that vulnerability is not cool, not safe. When we have the courage to lead with vulnerability, we can transform a team or culture. Those around us feel free to express an idea, a creative thought, or an intuitive flash.

Building better leaders

Leadership takes many forms and styles. You need not percolate with enthusiasm. You might be a quiet, strong leader who delivers a powerful energy, and you can be every bit as effective as the effusive leader. Your style doesn't diminish your impact. Just as each of us will be different when we are BIG, so each of us also will be different in our leadership. What is important is to play to your own strengths. That's how you can be the best leader possible.

In leading yourself first, small changes can have a huge impact. You can start with those and continue to build on them. You can work on your state of mind, putting yourself in an empowered state. You can work on building your personal brand and who you want to be and what your impact on others will be. You can work on the skills you need that will enhance that brand.

> **We all need to pursue work that we find meaningful and fulfilling and fun.**

Whatever you do, be intentional. Be what you intend to be. Go out into the world in full knowledge of yourself, ever mindful of those who are in the world with you. Know who is running the show, and dedicate yourself to silencing your Critic and amplifying your Whisperer. These are the elements of emotional intelligence.

We all need to pursue work that we find meaningful and fulfilling and fun. What we do should be a projection of ourselves, and as leaders we need to set the example for others that work is far from drudgery. We coach business leaders for professional excellence. We also help them tap into the fun and the fulfillment in work and in life. That's the triple-play of success. If work and career become a chore without meaning, it is hard to be a visionary leader.

The good news is that once you are in alignment with the true you, you break through to new possibilities. Others pick up on your example, and a new and exciting vibe can permeate the workplace. No longer on autopilot, you tune in to your values and vision and feel confident in communicating them.

Work can be play

As we discussed in Chapter 4, BIG is easy. Think of it as playing with positivity. That suggests that you get to do something, rather than that you have to do something— or need to do it, or should do it. "Play" connotes the ease and effortlessness that come in when you are BIG. You are curious about life and willing to experiment. You are not as concerned about getting it right and about whether it is working. The word suggests fun, innovation, and a childlike desire to experience new things. A child giggles while learning. Why can't we?

Some companies, such as Google and LinkedIn, now are paying their employees to play at work. They are doing that because research has shown that a playful mindset results in more innovation and creativity. Employees can play volleyball or scale a climbing wall. It lowers stress, boosts optimism, and increases motivation. People have long tended to believe that a real job is "all work, no play"—and that attitude, we are discovering, can reduce the amount of work that gets done.

We get a lot of pushback on the concept of work as play. "Wait a minute," people say. "That doesn't fit for us in our organization." It is gratifying to see research coming out about the advantages that best-in-class companies are finding when they foster that kind of environment. Some companies give employees an occasional day to work on whatever they please. They understand its role in success.

It's little wonder that many people have come to believe that American positivity and satisfaction have waned in recent years. Employee engagement has plummeted to only 30 percent, according to Gallup. We need to break free of the atmosphere of fear and doubt that prevails in so many workplaces and that has been accentuated as people have lost their jobs and the remaining employees have had to take on the tasks of two or more.

When you are BIG, work is play!

Where's your focus?

As we said before, what you focus on grows. When you are looking for what is right, you emphasize the fact that there's always a solution. When you focus on problems only, it's like a game of Whac-a-Mole™. You are smacking down trouble wherever it pops up. You feel that you are just doing what you must do, rather than celebrating what you get to do—and as a leader, your attitude, good or bad, spreads to your employees.

Dewitt Jones, a former photographer for *National Geographic*, has a beautiful way of illustrating the power of focusing on the positive in a video called *Celebrating What's Right With The World*. He tells how positivity infuses the ethic of *National Geographic*, and discusses how it has changed his life. Through the lens of his camera, he shows us how seemingly ordinary people and places—even disappointing ones—can radiate tremendous beauty if only we persist in asking ourselves, "What is right here? What can I celebrate?" and are patient enough to let answers surface. He calls it seeing the extraordinary in the ordinary and it's how he was able to focus in on the most amazing shots worthy of publication.

So it is for all of us, in the BIG picture. Within each of us, some part is great. That's where we need to focus. That's where we need to reframe, in a series of gradations leading us closer to BIG. As you zoom in on what matters most, you can see the possibilities. You move away from defensiveness, blame, and finger pointing. You move toward collaboration and teamwork. You know you're going to get your best shot yet.

"Nothing great was ever achieved without enthusiasm," wrote the essayist and poet Ralph Waldo Emerson. Or, as executive coach and speaker Grant Fairley put it, "A positive attitude may not solve every problem, but it makes solving every problem a more pleasant experience."

Curiosity as a cure

We gain so much through a mindset of curiosity. When you are BIG, your mind reaches out to ask questions about your world. You are open to possibilities. Never do you sit back and feel that you have it all figured out.

Some people are "knowers," and others are "learners." Knowers feel compelled to know the answer, a sign of an insecure ego. In today's world, of course, it's impossible for any one person, or any one leader, to know it all. Knowers operate more out of control than out of curiosity. With their directive approach, they do not really lead so much as they manage. It is a "Do what I say" style that stifles innovation. One could say that the old military model was built that way, and certainly organizations of decades ago often had that knower in the chair.

Today, we have many more lifelong learners with a predisposition to be curious. They have a healthy ego, so they have no problem saying, "I don't know the answer, but let's figure it out." They foster BIGness within the team, assuming a partnership that can take a more comprehensive look at situations. Employees feel empowered.

Millennials appreciate that kind of leadership, because they want to be invited to the table. They don't want their leaders talking down to them. When the leaders are learners, they foster an atmosphere of BIGness. They focus on working together. It all stems from that natural curiosity. By asking "what" and "how," leaders encourage more conversation—and more learning. More people get involved, and that is what sparks optimal operating states, producing compelling cultures.

> **When leaders know who they are when they are BIG—when they are curious and have a vision—the results are extraordinary.**

To see leaders making that shift is a profound experience.

When leaders know who they are when they are BIG—when they are curious and have a vision—the results are extraordinary. Ask yourself this: How much are you willing to cultivate the ideas of others, as a group, rather than thinking you have it figured out? Is there still room for curiosity in your world?

How you make them feel

"I've learned that people will forget what you said," said poet Maya Angelou, and "people will forget what you did, but people will never forget how you made them feel." Or as John Maxwell expressed it, "People don't care how much you know until they know how much you care."

> **Technical knowledge is important, but emotional intelligence is the heart of leadership.**

The art of communication is less about the words we say and far more about our nonverbal cues, our body language and tonality as well as our ability to understand our impact. We must keep that in mind when we think of the effect that leaders have on the culture of a company, or of a family, or a community.

Technical knowledge is important, but emotional intelligence is the heart of leadership. You need to know what makes people tick. A manager often puts the task ahead of the people and tends to dive in, instead of focusing on the development of people's abilities. A manager's attitude can be "heads down, and plow through," focusing on doing things right. Leaders are more "head up," with a focus of doing the right things.

On our journey of BIG, we are moving ever onward from "me" to "we." Once you have found within you the power to switch to a BIGger state, deliberately and intentionally, your newfound strength will have a ripple effect. You have led yourself first, ever curious and ever willing to learn. And now, with your ego in check and a positive attitude, you are jazzed to collaborate with others.

Primed for effective leadership, you are better able to guide a team. Your new priority is who you are together when you are BIG.

BIG INSIGHTS:

- What would be different if I led from my heart?

- What needs attention with those in my life who are "barely" or "brash," and how can I surround myself with more Bold Move makers?

- Where do I not allow myself to be vulnerable and what would happen if I did?

- What is one area of my life where I can stop "working" and start "playing"?

- What are the positives in any situation that I can focus on and grow?

- Where am I on the continuum of "Knower" vs. "Learner," and what do I need to calibrate for greater impact?

When I am BIG . . .

When I'm BIG, I have the mindset of David when he slew Goliath; "I can do all things through Christ who strengthens me" (Philippians 4:13). I am optimistic, fearless, brave, and have unquestionable and unshakeable belief and faith in what's possible. I can tackle any challenge (Goliath) in my life. Some people believe that the Goliaths in their life are too big to hit; when I'm playing BIG, I believe that they are too BIG to miss.

When I'm BIG, I am an inspiration to my family. I am a living and shining example of all that a man should be; God loving and God fearing; strong, meek, kind, caring, loving, vibrant, and courageous. I never give up nor do I give in to life's challenges. I give my family hope that being a good person will pay off in the long run. I love life and people and I live by the Golden Rule: "One should treat others as one would like others to treat oneself." I have benefited greatly by living by this rule.

When I'm BIG at work, I have the mindset of Denzel Washington in the movie Training Day, in the scene when he says, "King Kong ain't got nothing on me!" I am a leader, teacher, and student. I'm always challenging people to strive for higher levels of learning and education. I am a champion of diversity. I believe that the glass is always half full. I am inspiring and I give people hope. I don't allow anyone that is associated with me to quit or to give up. I am always leading and coaching.

When I'm BIG, *I am intellectually curious and an avid reader and learner. I am a student of leadership and of leaders; great leaders and the not so good ones, too. I am always looking for ways to grow personally and professionally. I am a student of life. I have a passion for life and all that it has to offer. I love nature and all that God has created. When I am BIG, I am being ME!*

That's who I am when I am BIG.

—HERBERT BILLINGER
VP of Franchise Operations
Einstein Noah Restaurant Group

CHAPTER 9

BIGGER: Who are WE when WE are **BIG**?

O ne of the more memorable expressions of BIG among boot camp participants was from an executive who concluded with, "most of all, when I'm BIG, I notice that everyone around me is BIG, too." He captured perfectly the point where "me" evolves into "we." It is the point where others around us are growing too.

Another executive who had used a coach on and off for several years was what you might call a "turnaround guy," in that he comes in to turn a company around and then finds himself out of work. He had come into a company that had recently emerged from bankruptcy— he was its fourth CEO in four years, and the people there were feeling beaten down. This company had faced serious compliance and financial issues and had significant customer complaints filed with the Better Business

Bureau and regulatory agencies. Sales were declining and the future still looked grim. They were really struggling and in desperate need of some great leadership with integrity, which this man offered. As a West Point graduate, integrity is ingrained in his brand.

He had two serious strikes against him with the skeptical employees. He was not from the industry and he hadn't been promoted from within. He feared they were essentially just waiting for the revolving door to swing again. It was imperative that he build trust and connection right from the start. On his management team were a few people who had come up through the blue-collar industry and a few others he called "white shirts," whom he had brought in from other big companies. The team needed to gel quickly. So, we did an executive retreat in which each person prepared an individual BIG statement, and then we focused on "Who are WE when WE are BIG?" We were looking for the view from the top of the mountain. Here is the BIG statement they created:

> *We have a crystal clear vision and strategy. We believe in the future. It's a partnership. We are the leader in the industry. We are pushing the envelope. We do the right things right. We are first class.*

We are respected. We consistently outperform the competition. We are coveted, envied. We are feared in the market by outsiders. We are revered by insiders. We are great corporate citizens.

We are innovators. We set the industry pace. We are overachieving and successful. We are relentless, we are fearless, we flawlessly execute. We are patient. We are realistic.

We are winners, we are inspirational, we are BIG. We are all-stars. We are champions. We are MVPs. We are on our game.

We are positive and optimistic. We are leaders, collectively and individually. We are friends, advisors, coaches, and mentors. We are united and cohesive. We are flexible and adaptable. We acknowledge one another. We are collaborative and complimentary. We are trusted to have the best interest at heart. We are bonded. We are invested in one another. We are approachable and available. We are dynamic. We are thriving. People like us.

And we are having fun.

We had already talked about their mission and their vision and their values. This exercise united them. The client went on to not only use that concept of BIG within the management team, but also at his in-store manager meetings and all-hands meetings. He also would use his personal BIG statement for new hire orientations and in various other places where it became an inspirational message to employees. And it was powerful; they turned the company around and ahead of schedule. Their financial results were soaring, the company culture was transformed, customer satisfaction levels skyrocketed, and within a year they received an A+ rating from the Better Business Bureau. They were named "Company of the Year" by the Association for Corporate Growth as the company that had done the best job of reinventing itself. It was a great win for everybody. It's interesting to note that five of the people from this small management team—over half—organically came together and are working with one another again in new company.

This can apply to teams of any sort that want to build their leadership. It can be an executive team or it can be just a department or committee, or it can be a sports team, or it can be a board of directors. It could be a sole entrepreneur. Or it could be a team of two working together, as we did as we collaborated on this book. It has brought out the best in both of us.

The BIG ripple effect

Dr. Fredrickson's research on positivity shows that when you focus on the positive, it creates an upward spiral of positivity. When a leader operates from a position of BIG, he or she creates a synergy. A positive ripple effect moves outward, influencing the culture of the team and organization. Have you ever met someone and noticed how your mood lifted? You felt inspired to be around that person and motivated to serve.

For years, a command-and-control type senior leadership team had run a distribution company. When the board brought in a new CEO who truly led with inspiration, curiosity, and vision, the results were impressive. After years of losing money, the company soon began to turn a profit. The new president operated from a place of positivity, was open to suggestions, and adopted a "we-based" culture of hope and possibility. The ripple effect of the new leadership moved throughout the organization. When senior leaders operate from BIG, then the benefits can extend all the way to the bottom line.

> **When a leader operates from a position of BIG, he or she creates a synergy. A positive ripple effect moves outward, influencing the culture of the team and organization.**

Leadership style clearly is what makes the difference. It is magical to see the shifts that happen with teams and companies when leadership operates from a BIG perspective. People want to be with leaders like that, who exude great confidence and inspiration.

Taking responsibility for the impact

We often learn of managers who are unaware of how their style of leadership has affected others. They come in, create a storm, and leave, oblivious to the bodies on the floor. Being BIG requires leaders to take responsibility for their impact and stick around to ensure that they motivated positive change and didn't just create a mess.

> *Being BIG requires leaders to take responsibility for their impact and stick around to ensure that they motivated positive change and didn't just create a mess.*

A senior team at a Fortune 200 company, known for its ability to get things done, was seen as brash in day-to-day exchanges. The team came to recognize, through coaching, how its management style affected others. Instead of barking orders and motivating by fear, the team members adopted a new style that was more collaborative and inviting. The old behavior of "Do as I say" with the tonality of a drill sergeant shifted to one of inquiry and positive motivation. Senior leaders strived to make sure their messages were received as intended.

It became a game changer. People could see the extra care that was being taken, and they could see that the senior leaders really did want to take responsibility for the way they communicated. Because the leaders were sticking around and observing their impact, they now had the opportunity to clean up any misread cues. The results were impressive. Employee engagement scores increased. The team's reputation turned around, and it became known as a top-performing team with great communications. People wanted to join the team, not leave it. And one more impressive benefit: The team did its job more effectively, with better results.

So often, we misread things. For example, one might say something to a colleague, who then feels attacked and becomes defensive. It would be easy to just blame him for taking it personally or know something wasn't quite right and just ignore it, or justify your behaviors by your good intentions or because of stress you are under. If you stick around to notice your impact, then you have a chance to clean it up and take responsibility for any miscommunication. When you do, you take a step toward improving the company, the team, and the culture. Once again, you are operating more in the "we" than in the "me." Your leadership is oriented toward serving others.

This is the style of leadership that focuses on social awareness and relationship management, weighing the impact on others. Such leaders are concerned about building connections and trust and intimacy over a longer term. They are keenly aware of the ripple effect of leadership, within companies, executive teams, and boards of directors, charitable organizations, and families. The question becomes one of collective identity—Who are WE when WE are BIG? When we are at our best, what does that look like?

The best teams ask questions

Dr. Fredrickson's work on positivity included a study on teams. The researchers watched teams from 600 companies, some high performing and some lower performing. They videotaped them and they watched how they interacted. They found that the members of teams from higher-performing companies demonstrated high connectivity to one another.

Those teams, in other words, were highly aware of the importance of relationship management. They showed a good deal of inquiry and a curiosity. Nobody was sitting there insisting that he or she had all the right answers.

They were learners, not knowers. They displayed a curious mindset, seeking out information, and looking outward as well as inward—outward at matters of reputation, and competition, and the customers.

The teams from the companies that did not perform as well, however, showed far less connectivity among the people around the conference tables. There was little curiosity in the room, with few questions, and it appeared that people were just waiting for a turn to talk. They showed almost no outward focus.

Helping others feel valued

"The most valued gift you have to offer is yourself," wrote business consultant and author Bob Burg in his book *The Go-Giver*. It is his "law of authenticity," one of his five principles for attaining "stratospheric success," and it is a principle quite relevant to the points we espouse in this book. Our most valued gift is not our knowledge, skill or effort. It's offering our true self to others. We must focus a lot less on "me" and much more on serving the "we."

Another of Bob Burg's principles is his "law of receptivity." "The key to effective giving is to stay open to receiving." Often, we have found that executives in transition feel vulnerable about their situation. They are encouraged when we remind them how good it felt in the past when they offered something of themselves by giving meaningful help to others in transition. If they got a lot of satisfaction from that, we tell them, then they should be pleased to let somebody else feel that way, too. They learn to stay open to receiving.

> **The nature of "we" leadership is to encourage and allow other people to feel valued, too.**

The nature of "we" leadership is to encourage and allow other people to feel valued, too. Some people are still hanging on to leading by their intellectual knowledge, or what they have to offer that they think is so much better than what everybody else has to offer. Our goal always must be inclusive and never divisive. We're all part of a team—the team of humanity, if you will. We're all in this together.

BIGGER INSIGHTS:

- What is possible if our team started playing BIGGER?

- What would be the ripple effect?

- Where can we start to take more responsibility for our impact as leaders?

- How can we ensure the people around us feel even more valued?

When I am BIG . . .

When I am BIG, I am connected to the present but rooted to grand possibilities. I am a wise energy—full of clarity, abundant with kindness, driven with passion.

When I am BIG, I am tethered to that moment when instinct (sense) and heart align. When I know I am in the moment and my reactions, thoughts, and responses are appropriate and my ideas are otherworldly.

When I am BIG, I am open wide but discerning. I see things clearly and manifest consciously.

When I am BIG, I am powerful but kind, a leader among leaders and a positive force for change. And growth. And wisdom.

—NEGAR AYROMLOO
CEO and Co-Founder
YourKidVid

CHAPTER 10

BIGGEST: The **BIG** ripple—a call to action

As we worked on this book together, we shared an experience—simple, yet moving—that we wish now to convey to you, our readers. Let us shift now to our individual voices to speak to you, our readers, about the experience:

Kimberly: As we were preparing to write these final chapters, I sent Allan a collection of the essays that my boot camp participants had written when asked, "Who are you when you are BIG?" I had shown him a handful of those in the past, but I think this bigger collection kind of took him to a different level of "wow."

Allan: Yes, it's one thing to talk about it, but this was the first time that I read one after another after another after another, and I found myself having just a really deep reaction to them—to the words, the intensity, the movement, the possibilities. These were people and leaders who, for the first time in their lives, were opening up and expressing something they hadn't really articu-lated before. We got on the telephone to talk about it. I said to Kimberly, "Talk to me about your boot camp experience, when you're asking people to stand up and share. What's it like for the people in the room? If just reading those BIG statements was intense for me, what must it be like for you, in person?"

> *I found myself having just a really deep reaction to them—to the words, the intensity, the movement, the possibilities.*

Kimberly: I told him that I got to experience that intensity every month. Allan asked me, "What is the feeling in the room when they read these?" I sipped my coffee, closed my eyes, and took myself back to the last boot camp, tapping into the experience as fourteen people found the courage to speak truthfully from the heart. I summoned words and phrases that seemed to capture the atmosphere. Allan recorded what I said:

It's like ...

- **Look out, world**
- **See me**

- **Hear me**
- **Feel me**
- **Vulnerability**
- **Courage**
- **Let's go**
- **Let's play**
- **Acknowledgment of one another**
- **Witnessing one another**
- **Nothing heavy**
- **Laughter**
- **Joy**
- **Peace**
- **Inspiration**
- **Calling forth**

I also spoke of the inviting ambience, in which everyone could feel BIG individually and call forth others around them to feel BIG—not in a pushy way, and not necessarily with words. It's just something that happens, I said, "So let's rise up together." Allan also recorded these words that I said, still deep in thought, recalling my last boot camp

> *The sun is shining on you to be seen, a spotlight of you on the stage—not in ego, but in the beauty of who you are as God's gift, loving yourself and letting the world watch.*

group: *The sun is shining on you to be seen, a spotlight of you on the stage—not in ego, but in the beauty of who you are as God's gift, loving yourself and letting the world watch.*

Allan: Then she opened her eyes. It had been cloudy when she closed them.

> **...but also to the human tribe, where everyone can feel activated into their BIGness.**

Kimberly: Yes, I was in Dallas, sitting outside on the patio of a friend's house, and it had been chilly and overcast when I closed my eyes. When I opened them, the sun was shining, and I immediately thought of Allan's long-ago dream that he had told me about—the one he had when he was a boy, and he dreamt he was on stage speaking to an audience of glowing hearts. I felt as if a spotlight had been turned on to shine down on what people had to say about being BIG.

Allan: The sun was coming out, a new brightness, just as I had seen years earlier on the San Francisco Bay Bridge as I awakened to the possibility that I could have a rewarding and fulfilling career if I had the courage to begin from the inside-out. Kimberly's words had me actually tapping into the wonder of how people were really seeing what might be possible for themselves. My thoughts turned not only to all those individuals with new possibilities, but also to the human tribe, where everyone can feel activated into their BIGness. It took me from sort of a myopic viewpoint to a macro viewpoint, to a worldview of the potentials for our planet, for our communities, and for our families.

> **There's vulnerability, but there's also courage. They're saying, "Let's go. Let's play!"**

Kimberly: Not only do I get to see each individual's magnificence emerge, but I also get to see the movement from "me" to "we," and I know from having observed our boot camp community the power of the ripple effect.

Allan: As Kimberly and I talked, we considered how we wanted to write these final pages. Where did we want our readers to be? How did we want to leave them as they closed the book? And it was clear: inspired, hopeful, and ready to go for it.

Kimberly: We felt we would be going far toward that end by sharing the feeling around the table at the boot camp, as each participant reads his or her BIG. The vitality lingers in the air, and builds in intensity from one reader to the next, until possibilities seem limitless. It's a collective feeling. Everybody in the room feels this. There's vulnerability, but there's also courage. They're saying, "Let's go. Let's play!" There's laughter, joy, peace. Inspiration gushes like a geyser and flows out in wide ripples.

BIG, BIGGER, BIGGEST

Once you become BIG, you become BIGGER as you practice it and live it, day in and day out. You become cognizant and intentional. You focus on strengths and learn how to manage the inner Critic. You see your own potential, and you put

> *And when you are BIG, you allow other people to be BIG around you.*

yourself in that BIG state repeatedly, as a matter of habit, because it feels so incredible to be there.

And when you are BIG, you allow other people to be BIG around you. That's even BIGGER. The "we" emerges in that room. Who are WE when WE are BIG? It's not just individuals anymore. As one person after another reads, you have inspiration on steroids. Every person feels not only called forth from what he or she has written, but called forth from what everybody else has written as well.

BIGGEST is the ripple effect—the effect that every BIG individual and every BIGGER team has in the world.

We need that human touch of one person encouraging another, who encourages yet another. The dream is that the human touch can go viral to make our world all that much better. And yet, as spiritual author and lecturer Marianne Williamson ob-

> **We need that human touch of one person encouraging another, who encourages yet another.**

served, it is that light that we most fear. In her words:

Our Deepest Fear

Our deepest fear is not that we are inadequate. Our deepest fear is that we are powerful beyond measure. It is our light, not our darkness, that most frightens us. We ask ourselves, "Who am I to be brilliant, gorgeous, talented, fabulous?" Actually, who are you not to be? You are a child of God. Your playing small does not serve the world. There is nothing enlightened about shrinking so that other people won't feel insecure around you. We were all meant to shine as children do. We were born to make manifest the glory of God that is within us. It's not just in some of us; it's in everyone. And as we let our own light shine, we unconsciously give other people permission to do the same. As we are liberated from our own fear, our presence automatically liberates others.

—Marianne Williamson
from *A Return to Love: Reflections on the Principles of A Course in Miracles*

There is no glory in keeping ourselves down. We must shine, brilliantly, so that we can free others to shine around us. We must find light where there was darkness. We must live from the heart—the very root of courage.

As coaches, we are still learning. We are still reaching for the next Bold Move. We want to spread the word about the power within each of us if we reach for our potential. We feel that this message is so BIG that it must be spread on a grander scale to serve more people.

> **We're all in this together, and we cannot serve the world by thinking small.**

This has to grow. It's too important not to grow. It's time to take center stage on this conversation. It is time to go global, and we would like to be stewards for that transition. As we have called others to play BIG, we must continue to answer that call ourselves. But in doing so, we lay down our egos. We need your help. We're all in this together, and we cannot serve the world by thinking small.

This book has focused on the executive leaders with whom we deal daily and who have the wherewithal to advance a movement. As we have demonstrated, however, these principles apply to the dynamics and structures of all organizations, and families, and communities. And so to our readers, we call you forth. Join us and the BIG movement at www.GettingToBIG.com where you will find tools and resources to:

Be BIG

Live BIG

Lead BIG!

Courageously release what already lies within you. Join us to inspire even more BIGness in the world!

BIGGEST INSIGHTS:

- What if each of us was released of our fear and allowed ourselves to be powerful beyond measure?

- What would a collective uprising of BIG mean for my company, my family, my community?

- What actions will I take now to make the world BIGGER?

Magnificence emerging

by Kimberly Roush

I couldn't finish this book without sharing what has taken place in my world since Allan and I began writing this book in 2013. As we mentioned earlier, Allan and I have both participated in a yearlong program called Co-Active Leadership, offered by The Coaches Training institute (CTI). Allan completed the program fifteen years before I did.

The program is a series of four weeklong retreats, described in the book *The Stake: The Making of Leaders* by Henry Kimsey-House, co-founder of CTI, and David Skibbins. I enrolled hoping to take my business to the next level—and then life showed up!

Shortly after the first retreat, my brother surrendered to his alcoholism and checked into the Betty Ford Center for sixty days of rehab—an incredible Bold Move. He has a college degree and had chosen the construction field, where he felt drinking every day after work was normal. He'd been exposed to that even as a young boy. It was a forty-year-old habit that had taken its toll.

I'm pleased to acknowledge that the release of this book coincides with the one-year anniversary of his sobriety. I am so proud of him, and the Leadership program allowed me to play BIG in serving him.

I had just begun the retreat when my brother first started talking about going to rehab. Members of my "tribe" supported me in such an incredible way in helping me to understand what he was going through. The program and my tribe allowed nothing short of multiple miracles to align the stars around his recovery. Before the third week of his rehab, which is family week at Betty Ford, all my codependent behaviors were raging out of control. I was being a brash move maker on steroids. My behaviors came not from my heart but rather from fear. The program and my tribe mates again helped me find the courage to make changes in my family relationship that were long overdue. I feel like I was able to join him in his journey of "rehabilitation" and bring myself "back to a good or healthy state" within my family life. It was a part of our lives where we previously had both been playing small, making only "barely" moves.

My brother came to stay with us for a few weeks after

rehab, and within days I departed for my second Leadership retreat. It was there that I learned to think of intimacy as "in to me see." The concept teaches us to understand ourselves and one another, and to connect closely in a way that promotes powerful leadership together.

When I returned from that retreat, I felt that I had better tools to better see into myself, into my brother, and into all of my relationships. It was at the retreat that I learned to think of courage as a "heart rage," and I have been able to find the courage to be BIG when life is scary.

The third and fourth retreats have built on those concepts and helped me move from "me" to "we," and take responsibility for my impact. They also challenged me to make this book my "Leader Quest" and build on the experience with my brother to make this project even richer.

My brother and I have talked about who he is when he is BIG. I have learned that the things we make hard become so much easier when you are BIG, and I have seen this also be true for him as I have witnessed his magnificence emerging. Confronting his addiction to alcohol allowed him to find his BIG. He's full of life and he fairly quickly landed a rewarding six-figure job doing what he loves. He's always been an inspiration to me throughout my life, and now he is an even greater inspiration. He is proof to me that believing in yourself and perhaps something a little greater than yourself will always bring out the BIG in a person. B-I-G—Believing in Greatness.

I feel called forth to play even BIGGER in this world. Let us be BIG together.

ABOUT THE AUTHORS

Allan Milham, Master Certified Coach (MCC), and **Kimberly Roush**, Professional Certified Coach (PCC), are among the industry's most elite. Together, they represent nearly a quarter-century of experience coaching top performing executives.

Before following their passion into coaching, both spent over two decades in corporate America, Allan as a consultant in both the human resources and career management industries and Kimberly as a national partner in Big-Four public accounting.

In addition to their coaching practices, they are both keynote speakers and leadership facilitators. They are members of the International Coach Federation and the National Speakers Association.

**Visit us at www.GettingToBIG.com
and join our BIG community!**
Register your book and receive access
to free resources including:

The 60-minute
The Impact of BIG
author interviews with executives highlighted in the book

Join the on-line BIG Discussion by:
Joining our mailing list at www.GettingToBIG.com
Liking us on Facebook at
www.facebook.com/gettingtoBIG
Following us on Twitter at @GettingToBIG
Follow us on Google+ at
www.google.com/+Gettingtobignow

For information on bulk purchases for
your company or your team,
please email info@GettingToBIG.com

**Contact Allan or Kimberly directly to
learn more about these services:**
Executive Coaching
Keynote Speaking
Facilitated Leadership and Teambuilding Workshops

Allan Milham
Bold Moves Enterprises, Inc.
Allan@GettingToBIG.com
(301) 530-0008

Kimberly Roush
All-Star Executive Coaching
Kimberly@GettingToBIG.com
(714) 283-3840

CPSIA information can be obtained
at www.ICGtesting.com
Printed in the USA
BVHW041430190819
556214BV00027B/2794/P

9 781599 324555